everything went on at
THE ROUND HOUSE

a hundred years of the Manchester University Settlement

MICHAEL E ROSE & ANNE WOOD

1995

© UNIVERSITY OF MANCHESTER

ISBN 0 906107 44 X

Printed and Bound by:-
MFP DESIGN & PRINT
Longford Trading Estate
Thomas Street
Stretford
Manchester
M32 0JT

Front Cover illustration by:-
L.S.LOWRY - 1930

I am proud to be President of the Manchester University Settlement in its Centenary Year.

I first joined the committee of the Settlement in 1982 and became President in 1989. I had of course been aware of its existence and the splendid work it had done in the past, but it was not until I joined the committee that I fully appreciated the dedication and application of its staff, over-worked and short of funds, in tackling the many tasks that the Settlement undertook.

It is that dedication and selflessness was well as the importance of its role in the community that makes the successful continuation of the work of the Settlement so vital.

I hope that with the support and goodwill of all who know its worth, the Settlement may have the necessary backing to allow it to have a future that will live up to its proud past.

John B Zochonis
President

ACKNOWLEDGEMENT

The authors would like to thank all those who contributed their memories and their photographs to this book. Without their help, it would not have been possible.

CONTENTS

Ancoats from the air - taken in the 1950s before the demolition of the 1960s

"EVERYTHING WENT ON AT THE ROUND HOUSE"

A HUNDRED YEARS OF MANCHESTER UNIVERSITY SETTLEMENT 1895 - 1995

Chapter One

Ancoats in 1895 was not a desirable place in which to settle. A community on Manchester's eastern side, its few hundred acres were bounded by the Oldham Road to the north and the River Medlock to the south, whilst Great Ancoats Street and the township boundary of Newton Heath formed its western and eastern limits respectively. Created in the early 19th century by industry's need to house its workforce close to their places of work, it was described by Friedrich Engels in 1844 as the "New Town" or "Irish Town" of Manchester. By 1851, it housed a population of 54,000 and exceeded in size industrial towns such as Bury or Wigan. Unlike them, however, it lacked the shape and amenities of a separate town, consisting as it did of rows of houses, often back to back, run up hastily to accommodate a young immigrant workforce. No consideration had been given to community needs in its building. Cramped housing competed, often unsuccessfully, for space with cotton mills, iron foundries, coal wharves and slaughter houses. By the end of the century, this new community had settled down. Manchester had provided its New Cross Ward with the most urgent needs of paving, drainage and water supply. Churches, chapels, shops, schools and public houses had appeared to serve the spiritual, educational and material needs of Ancoats people. It remained however a dreary place, soot begrimed and smoke polluted.

"Some of them could not live or sleep in Ancoats until Manchester has been made less of a cinder heap," the eccentric Manchester Socialist, Charles Rowley,

BEGINNINGS

himself an Ancoats boy, told a meeting of students, academics and professional men and women in 1895.

Rowley was wrong. The meeting at which he delivered his warning, on March 27th, 1895, agreed to establish a university settlement residence in Manchester with Ancoats as its location. On October 4th, 1895, its first two residents Miss C.H. Stoehr, a botanist, and Dr. Annie Anderson M.D. walked "under the Railway Bridge, up the Hill, over the cobbles, round the curve of a treeless drive, and into the temple of arts and crafts," Ancoats Hall, formerly

the seat of the Mosley family, lords of the manor of Manchester. The first university settlement in an English city outside London had been founded.

Despite its drab appearance, Ancoats itself was by 1895 a centre of social experiment. Ten years earlier the wealthy paper manufacturer, Thomas Coglan Horsfall had leased Ancoats Hall for the site of his Ancoats Art Museum designed to bring painting, sculpture and other things of beauty to the people of treeless Ancoats. Charles Rowley, despite his doubts about sleeping in Ancoats, took its New Islington

Ancoats Hall - site of T.C.Horsfall's Art Museum, and one of the Settlement's residences until the 1960s.

young, to live in a working class district on the same street as working people. Close contact would create understanding. Settlement residents would experience at first hand the problems of their neighbours. They would cease to think of working people as feckless, drunken and ignorant. Working class neighbours would visit the settlement house and come to appreciate the life lived there. They too might change their ideas of the rich as idle people who spent their lives eating and drinking. A neighbourly community of all classes would be formed. Ancoats would become capable of making its influence felt both in civic and in national life.

Star Hall - a religious mission and settlement in Ancoats opened by the wealthy industrialist, Francis Crossley. In 1891 Crossley and his wife moved into Star Hall.

This had been the idea of the Reverend Samuel Barnett, an East London clergyman, who founded, with support from the Universities of Oxford and of

Hall as the base for his Ancoats Brotherhood, which organised lectures, concerts, rural excursions and other events, aimed at bringing cultural inspiration to the inner city. Another wealthy Mancunian, the engineer, Francis Crossley, had come to live at Star Hall, Ancoats and established it as a centre for missionary work. The new university settlement combined in some ways the aims of these earlier institutions. Like the Art Museum, to which it was joined between 1900 and 1919, it aimed to provide cultural experiences for those who lacked them; like the Ancoats Brotherhood it sought to provide discussion on all manner of issues especially those which might improve the lives of Ancoats people; like Star Hall, it had a mission, not to preach a particular gospel but to bring educated middle class people, especially the

Rev. Samuel Barnett - Warden of Toynbee Hall, Whitechapel and founding father of the settlement house movement.

9

BEGINNINGS

Oxbridge in East London - Toynbee Hall, opened 1884. A purpose built settlement house, Toynbee Hall was designed by the architect, Elijah Hoole.

Cambridge, what was probably the world's first settlement house, Toynbee Hall, in the Commercial Road, Whitechapel in 1884. This example was rapidly followed in east and south London where numerous settlements sprang up over the next ten years. Exported to the United States, the idea took root and 74 settlement houses had been founded by 1897, the majority of them in Boston, New York and Chicago.

Scotland also proved receptive and the Universities of Edinburgh and Glasgow were both supporting settlements by 1890. English cities however failed to catch the spark. As a result, Samuel Barnett, together with the eminent Conservative politician, Sir John Gorst, who had recently visited the flourishing settlements in the United States, began a series of missionary visits to English cities early in 1895.

Manchester was his first port of call. He and Gorst spoke at a meeting in Owens College Union on March 27th, 1895. He found a ready reception for his idea from philanthropists like Horsfall and Rowley, from academics like Owens Principal, Adolphus Ward, Samuel Alexander, Professor of Philosophy and Thomas Frederick Tout, Professor of History and from senior students like Pilkington Turner and Woodroofe Fletcher who had for some years been urging the college to become more involved with the community surrounding it. A resolution to found a settlement was passed. T.C. Horsfall chaired a committee to carry out the resolution and offered Ancoats Hall, his Art Museum, as a base for its activities. Miss Stoehr and Dr. Anderson walked up the treeless drive. The rest is this history.

20. Every Street, originally the men's residence of the Settlement, it adjoined the Round House

In July 1896, the Settlement's First Annual General Meeting approved the name of the association as "The University Settlement, Manchester," and produced a mission statement. The Settlement was "Founded in the hope that it may become common ground on which men and women of various classes may meet in goodwill, sympathy and friendship, that the residents may learn something of the conditions of an industrial neighbourhood and share its interests, and endeavour to live among their neighbours a simple and religious life." The desire to mix the classes did not of course extend to one to mix the sexes. Female residents under Miss Stoehr lived in a house in Ardwick until the facilities at Ancoats Hall were brought up to the standards required for young ladies. Male residents under Ernest Campagnac, an Oxford graduate, were housed separately, also in Ardwick. An Ardwick University Settlement seemed likely. The women, however, by now under the dynamic leadership of Alice Crompton, returned to Ancoats Hall in 1898. The men took over 20, Every Street, Ancoats, a terraced house which had briefly been an experimental working men's college, Ruskin Hall. Behind this Every Street residence was the famous Round Chapel of the early 19th century doctor and Chartist sympathiser, James Scholefield. In 1900, with a donation of £2,000 from Mrs. Worthington, the Settlement purchased the graveyard of the Round Chapel, which it turned into a playground, and the adjacent Recreation Hall. The chapel itself, disused and derelict by the 1920s,

Chapter Two

PLACES

The Round House
(1958), before and
after (opposite) the
resurfacing of the
playground by
an International
Work Camp.

was rescued with the aid of a bequest to the Settlement from a wealthy Altrincham woman, Alice Bickham. Refurbished and opened in June 1928, it was christened the Round House. From then on it vied with Ancoats Hall as the centre of Settlement activities, and brought in useful revenue when space in it was let to other organisations. In Helen Pilkington's woodcut and L.S. Lowry's later drawing, it became a symbol of the Settlement.

"The Round House had this beautiful maple floor - me and Mrs. Kirkmam used to polish it. You could dance on it. The kids ruined it you see when they shut it up. There was a stage and all in the same room." (Flo Beddows).

Use of Ancoats Hall continued long after the separation of the Settlement and the Art Museum in 1919, although its art collection was later removed by the city's education committee. Renovated in 1946, to provide accommodation for the Warden, Ralph Reedman and his family, the Hall became the main location for both male and female residence after 1949, when a new Warden, Gordon Kidd, moved into the Round House. There continued to be, according to the warden's wife, " a good deal of to-ing and fro-ing between the two buildings" after that. The decline of residence in the early 1960's, however, led to the decision to give up the tenancy of the Hall in 1963. Its owners, the British Transport Commission, who had inherited it from the L.M.S Railway Company, had decided to try to sell it in 1962, and it was later demolished, a fate which was to befall the Round House, despite its listed status, in 1986.

Even in the late 1920's when the Round House was first refurbished, there were signs of change in Ancoats and other inner city districts as substandard

PLACES

1930s Ancoats - corner of White Street near settlement. The boarded up shop indicates the beginnings of slum clearance.

In 1931, two houses, numbers 5 and 7, Surbiton Road, were leased on the poorer Newton Heath estate and a variety of activities launched by the four residents of them. In 1934, another settlement resident, Miss Pollard, moved into a flat at Kennet House, a new block of municipal flats in Smedley Lane. In 1940, despite the outbreak of war, three shop fronts and a flat were rented in Stanley Grove, Gorton, as the base for another satellite settlement. The Guild of Neighbours established at Newton Heath folded in 1943, whilst the Gorton premises were

The First Step Out of Manchester. 34, Tarporley Avenue today. Rented by the Settlement in 1928 to serve the Wilbraham Estate, it became the base for Emity Jenkinson's Wilbraham Association.

housing was demolished, and its residents given the opportunity of moving to new council houses or flats further out of the city. Manchester University, like many other inner city settlements, faced the dilemma of remaining with a dwindling number of neighbours in Ancoats or moving to new estates which, despite their higher quality houses, lacked the communal premises and activities which a settlement could provide. With the settlement zeal for experiment, Manchester did both.

In 1928, it rented 34, Tarporley Avenue on the Wilbraham estate as a residence for women workers. A hut to house community activity was erected in Hart Road and a self governing Wilbraham Association developed under the leadership of Emily Jenkinson.

Settlement flat in Starr Avenue, Gorton, decorated for the visit of Princess Elizabeth and Prince Phillip - 1949.

given up in the late 1940's and much of the work there taken over by the Save the Children Fund. The Settlement however continued its presence by renting a flat in a newly opened block in Starr Avenue.

"I think they were three storey flats and the settlement was allowed to rent one of the flats, the idea being that a group of students would live there and they would raise the social standing of the people in the flats - an awful thing really wasn't it? I can quite assure you that the students kept their house in a far worse state than most of the people in Starr Avenue." (Kathleen Kidd).

The 1960s saw the rapid wholesale clearance of much of Manchester's inner city. By 1969, plans for an inner ring road threatened to isolate Every Street from its community. It was decided to relocate in the Hulme or Moss Side areas. Two houses in Moss Lane

Settlement Outposts - 5 & 7, Surbiton Road, Newton Heath, (above) and (below) 170, Stanley Grove, Gorton, as they are today

PLACES

402 MOSS LANE EAST
NEIGHBOURHOOD
NURSERY

400 MOSS LANE EAST
HEATHERBANK
COMMUNITY HOUSE

398 AND 396 MOSS LANE EAST
CHILDREN'S ART CENTRE
AND
ADMINISTRATIVE OFFICE

East were purchased in 1971. In Beswick, to the east of the city, the old St. Aidan's Rectory in Bosworth Street was rented.

"*The old building was very run down. It was very full of character - lots of rooms. Young people were involved in doing a lot of painting of the building. They decorated their rooms how they would like them to be with some support and it was very homely, very nice. It was very welcoming to young people. I don't think it was so welcoming to adults. It was very good for multi-use, very good as a youth centre - a bit like Aladdin's Cave. It was a bit like a cave, but the children used to help with suggestions as to how they would like it to look so they would respect the place.*" (Marie Williamson)

In 1973, after nearly eighty years, the Settlement left Every Street and relocated at Heatherbank House on Moss Lane East. Two adjacent houses were added and extensive renovation began. Unfortunately, just as the new location was taking shape, the Settlement ran into a major financial crisis. In 1977, Heatherbank House and the adjacent properties were sold to the city, and the Settlement's work concentrated in Beswick. For all its "Aladdin's Cave" excitement, however, the old rectory proved expensive to maintain and unsuitable for many types of work. Financial support from the Greater Manchester Council and a generous donation from John Zochonis enabled the demolition of the old rectory and the erection on its site of a plain, single storey brick building, Aidans,

"A bit like Aladdin's cave ". The old St Aidan's Rectory. Bosworth Street, Beswick.

opened in 1983. In the same year, the empty Round House passed into the hands of the G.M.C. and fell under the bulldozer, three years later. For all the ambiguity as to whether its design is that of a community centre or a base for community workers, Aidans is the first purpose built building in the Settlement's hundred year history. It takes over the role of its distinguished predecessors as a fortress of hope on the frontiers of despair.

PLACES

Aidan's -
an artist's impression.

*"***M***r. Woods, I do not believe in geographical salvation,"* the eminent American settlement worker, Jane Addams, is said to have reproved a colleague, overanxious to define the exact boundaries of a settlement neighbourhood. The story of its buildings and the locations they occupied is only the background to the story of this, or any settlement. Its real history is that of the people who used the buildings.

a. Children

Children were always to the fore in settlement history. The first residents found that although adult neighbours might at first treat them with reserve as part of another mission come to preach or institution to control, children were less inhibited. Natural curiosity brought them to the door of the settlement house. An invitation to come in and to have their own space and play equipment was a tempting one which often overcame the reservations instilled in them by their elders and betters.

"Before they left the museum, Miss Hindshaw asked the boys if they'd like to go to a Christmas party at the Round House. There would be carol singing and Santa Claus and a present for each one of them. They said "Yes, please Miss" and she said they would have to take part in a little nativity play which would be good fun.

Chapter Three

The boys had to give careful consideration to this condition for Catholics were not supposed to get involved with the goings-on at the University Settlement - where they would have to mix with Protestants. And then had not both Father Sullivan and Father Granelli told the children that it was enough to have a model crib in the church at Christmas without cavorting on a stage? But the thought of a present from Father Christmas persuaded them, within half a second, to agree. (Malcolm Lynch, *The Streets of Ancoats* 1985 p41).

The earliest annual reports of the Settlement list boys' and girls' clubs, children's concerts and children's parties high on the programme of activities. "The pleasantest parties," the First Annual Report of 1897 recorded, "were those for children." Many of them, it continued, "were quite at home here, and through them the acquaintance of their parents is often most easily made."

Seventy years later, Marie Williamson had the same experience.

"I used to work a lot with families when I first came, giving them general support and advice. They learned where to get help through the children coming."

Not that in the early days, the children's coming was value free. The language of the early reports suggests that proper standards of behaviour were expected, though these were not obtained without

some effort on the part of those who ran the children's activities. The organisers of the Girls' Club in 1898 noted that "the improvement in the behaviour of the girls has been maintained but there is still something left to be desired," whilst in 1900, the Little Girls' Club was meeting on three evenings a week for "sewing, drilling, dancing, knitting, singing and at the same time teaching them gentleness, order and neatness." The Boys' Club of the same year had "excellent youngsters full of grit and cuteness," but more space was needed for its 55 members as "a one room boys' club must try the patience of the most nerveless."

Work with children had its serious, educational

Street Play in Ancoats c.1906 (right) and c.1960 (left). The Settlement aimed to provide an alternative to this. Children probably took advantage of both alternatives.

side and in this the close relationship between the Settlement and the Art Museum also located in Ancoats Hall was of great importance. In the year of the Settlement's birth T.C. Horsfall had obtained an amendment of the Education Code to allow schoolchildren to visit museums and galleries in school hours as part of their education. The appointment of Bertha Hindshaw in 1912 as a settlement resident and curator of the Art Museum brought to Ancoats an enthusiast keen to enrich children's lives with the inspiration of great art. This was not without its embarrassments.

"The poor lad wished the floor would open up and swallow him when he stepped into the room. The whole place was very rude. He had never seen the like before. It was filled with large plaster statues and most of them had no clothes on at all. One man had a leaf where there should have been something else; and there was a naked lady with an arm gone. Miss Hindshaw told them they'd all been gods before the birth of Jesus." (Malcolm Lynch, *The Streets of Ancoats* 1985 p40-41).

Sometimes participation seemed a high price to pay.

"We made a record of carols. The idea was to take the record with us and go and sing in hospital wards and we did. We went to Ancoats Hospital. The idea was to go in, put the record on and sing along with it. He was a very old man. He had us in there about two or three times a week at night. We'd go and do this practice. We'd do this when we went to the youth club. We'd go in and what we really wanted was the records and to be
where the boys were and watching the fencing or table tennis. But we felt we really had to go because he wanted this choir and he never really got anyone. We felt then that he really relied on us and although we didn't really want to do it - singing these songs - we'd all be standing round the piano and pushing one another but you felt he would be so disappointed. So we had the feelings then." (Jacky Homer).

Despite these cultural requirements, Ancoats children were not deterred. The Settlement provided visions of a privileged childhood which Ancoats children were eager to glimpse.

"When I was very young and went to the Settlement after school, they had rooms full of lots of bricks and dolls' houses - big houses - I remember that. The dolls' house mesmerised me because it had the real miniature little things, you know. I used to set it all up and hope that no-one would come and get it." (Jacky Homer).

"We used to do handicrafts. We used to make pictures out of silver paper. The teachers used to do the glass with black paint on the back and draw a crinoline lady and we used to fill it in with coloured paper and glue. I made loads of them. I don't know what happened to them. My mum must have thrown them out. We used to do sewing and knitting. That was in the winter. In the summer, we'd be out in the yard playing all sorts of things. I learned to play tennis there." (Joan Seaton).

Demand to join in such activities was high, and membership frequently had to be rationed for lack of space.

"We had a terrific problem because of the size of the Round House. I ran Junior Girls. We had a hundred Junior Girls at night. We had to bar the door because we couldn't take all of them. We had a playcentre which had 50 or 60 in at a time. We had a youth club again with 50 or 60 and when we had our Christmas party, it would go up to 100.". (Kathleen Kidd. 1950's).

In 1965, St. Mary's rectory was leased from the city as a children's play centre when the numbers became too great for the Round House, and later

A Day in the Park. - Settlement Play Scheme in Heaton Park. 1960s.

that year there was talk of buying All Souls School building for use as a play centre. At about the same time a play scheme was launched in Heaton Park and by the summer of 1967 this was attracting as many as 600 children.

Space for play was something that settlement workers thought was lacking in overbuilt Ancoats. As

Playground outside the Round House c.1905. By providing dedicated play space, Settlement workers aimed to keep children from the dangers of playing in busy streets or near canals

soon as money became available, therefore, the Settlement acquired the graveyard of Scholefields Round Chapel and equipped it with swings and other items of play equipment. Its successor in the 1970's was the adventure playground which Marie Williamson remembers behind St. Aidans's Rectory.

"There was quite a bit of land at the back so we had a kind of adventure playground at the back as well which we built in the summer and we had a huge bonfire at the end. It was built mainly by volunteers. It wasn't a big adventure playground, just small structures, a platform and a few planks - nothing very elaborate but quite solid. We also used to do a lot of painting and painting the structures outside and we'd play outside games. We had a trampoline and sometimes we'd go outside if the weather was good." (Marie Williamson).

Although such playgrounds provided a place of safety compared to busy and dangerous streets, children were still exposed to the smoke and grime of

"We had a kind of adventure playground at the back as well which we built in the summer and we had a huge bonfire at the end ".
Aidan's Adventure Playground. - 1970s

Ancoats. To take them away from these if only briefly in the summer months, supporters of the Settlement were encouraged to invite parties of Ancoats children to their homes in south Manchester's more salubrious suburbs for an afternoon of play and fresh air in their gardens. Even these places, however, had their perils.

"They took me to one doctor's house in Didsbury and they gave me hockey stick, golf stick and a ball. Now, there was an alsatian chained up in the garden and we was told to keep away from him. but,

unfortunately the ball I was knocking went near the dog so I started reaching with the stick. I couldn't reach so I moved forward. As I moved forward, the dog thought I was going to crack it. There are scars where it bit me face open - see? It bit all me face open". (Mr. Lawlor 1936 - 1938).

There were risks on both sides.

"In the afternoon, they used to take a party out to Professor Simon's estate. The kids from Ancoats weren't used to this. They used to send the butler out with cream cakes for all of us. The poor butler used to get raided with cream cakes. The kids had never seen a cream cake - they didn't know what a cream cake was. They didn't eat the cakes, they just hit the butler with them. He never had a chance. We had a heck of a time saying "Don't do that!" It was hilarious." (Stanley Heath 1930's).

By 1918, these suburban outings were being organised on a more formal basis. An agreement with Cavendish School in Didsbury led to groups of children being taken from Ancoats to a vacation school in the Cavendish buildings. The Tramways Department provided free tram rides to take the children to and from Didsbury. Even this did not really create equality of opportunity between Ancoats children and the more privileged who by the early 1900's had come to expect a seaside or country holiday in the summer as a break from the routines of home and school. After the First World War, the Settlement began to organise camping holidays in Derbyshire or on the North Wales coast, and for many children these proved the most memorable of Settlement activities.

Children boarding the free tram to take them to the summer holiday school at the Cavendish School, Didsbury. - 1935

"Did we benefit from the experience? Well it was the first time that I had been away from my parents and home. I learnt that I could cope with that. It took us away from the mean inner city streets and gave us clean seaside air. We were cared for and provided for by people we didn't know and who didn't know us. It was a forerunner of evacuation which was to follow a few years later." (Mr. Carroll - of Birkdale Camp, Southport).

In 1930, the Settlement obtained "three acres of wind-swept earth's surface" at Ludworth, near Marple and on it erected a hut, the gift of Mr. and Mrs J. Todd and called the Douglas Hut in memory of their son, a Manchester University medical student. This provided a base for camps and day outings.

"We used to go to Marple. The Ludworth Hut. Stirrup Benches was the name of the little area the hut was in.

"Three acres of wind swept earth's surface, within easy distance of Marple Bridge Station, " The Douglas Hut, Ludworth under reconstruction by Quaker Volunteers in 1961; and (below) an earlier view.

It was a real holiday for us. I know it was only Marple which is only up the road but to us then it was a long way. We used to go on the train, go into Marple and take the bus from Marple to Stirrup Benches. Then we'd set off walking up this hill and boy was it a hill? It was wonderful. It was at the top of a hill and it was a massive wooden hut. There was one great big living room with two big long tables and seats. There was one bedroom at one end with bunk beds in and there was a bedroom at the other end. Very often, if it wasn't being used, they'd allow my dad and the family to go and have a holiday there." (Joan Seaton).

Television and the motor car has perhaps made an outing to Marple a little less of an adventure in recent

dormitories and a large room at the bottom. A lot of the places had big grounds which we used a lot. Then we used Scottish National Camps later on which was a different kind of holiday as everyone was in units. All the groups were in their own little bungalow and there was a large room for coming together to do arts and crafts and games and another area for eating. When we had no money one time we did a camp for 40 at a time on Anglesey which was horrendous." (Marie Williamson).

An early concern of the settlement was for children with physical disabilities, "cripples" in the harsh Victorian term. By 1898, settlement reports refer to the holding of Santa Fina parties by Helen Fisher, a young graduate resident, for disabled children. Rejecting the word, "cripple", she called

times, but the organisation of holidays and vacation play schemes for children remained a central feature of the settlement's work.

"We took them to Silverdale with Ken Walmsley, he was a blind lad. We took them to Silverdale for a weekend and it was wonderful to see them jumping in the channel. They jumped and ran in the water and played. We used to take them hiking, me and the blind lad in one of the worst winters we've ever had 62/63. Once he fell so far down in a snowdrift that we had to dig him out with our hands. You wouldn't be allowed to do it today. But they loved it." (Eric Youd).

"We used a place in the Lake District quite a lot then (1970's). Alston Boarding School in Carlisle and Lime House, beautiful old building. There was a place in Cheshire near Nantwich. It was a huge house with

her organisation after an Italian girl, Fina de Ciardi, whose endurance of physical suffering had earned sainthood. Helped by the historian, R.C.K. Ensor, whom she later married, Helen Fisher discovered and mapped out the homes of all disabled children within a three quarter mile radius of Ancoats Hall. Santa Fina provided activities to end their isolation and lobbied for recognition of their special educational needs. In the best settlement tradition, this local work spread city wide, and a special school was opened in 1911. Two years later, Manchester's Education Committee which had been watching Santa Fina's

Camp on Anglesey - 1970s

PEOPLE

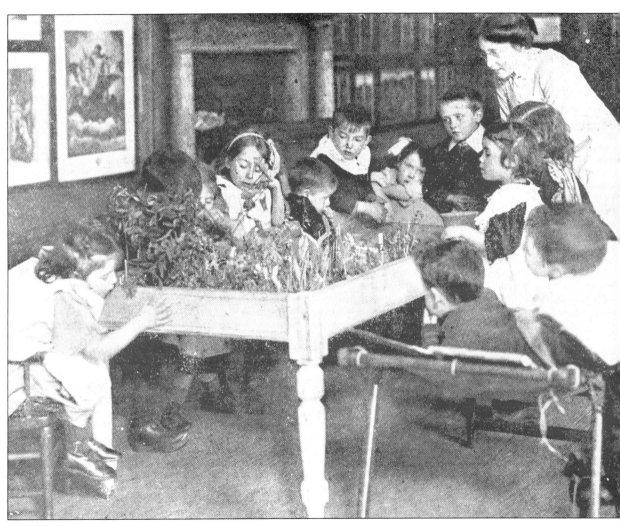

work with interest took over the school. Santa Fina continued its other work, providing holidays, clothing and bath chairs for children, and organising handicraft classes and a penny savings bank. In 1913, it affiliated to the Invalid Childrens' Aid Association, and became a separate movement with its own history.

b. Youth

Like churches and other organisations, the settlement workers found that childish enthusiasm could be replaced by youthful indifference once the early teens were reached and the important rite of passage from school child to young worker was made.

"All this ceased when I was 14 and left school. It would never have done to play in the street when you were a worker, any more than you would be expected to go for your own chips. I remember clearly this Rites of Passage when for the first time a younger child was sent for the chips and peas for my tea. A great moment." (Helen Wood).

In the early years, the Settlement took over the

A rival attraction? - Worker's dance during dinner hour at an Ancoats cotton mill. - 1926

"The intermingling of age groups". Christmas social in the 1950s.

running of a Lads' Club in the Jersey Street Dwellings, although club leaders complained that night shift working made the lads' attendance irregular. A young school teacher, Eva Gore Booth, organised a Young Women's Social Evening out of which developed a dramatic society, the Ancoats Elizabethan Society, whose ambitious mission was "a revival of the dramatic spirit, Elizabethan in the boldness of its aim and its independence of nineteenth century machinery." A Senior Girls' Club was formed to link the Little Girls' Club with the adult activities of the Settlement, although "the economy practised by some of the girls

with regard to soap and water" caused distress to some of the lady volunteers who ran the club. At the same time, members of the Boys' Reading Class were given the opportunity to progress to the Youths' Fiction Reading Circle. A Junior Associate Members Group for 16 to 30 year olds was founded in 1926, by which time the Settlement was co-operating with the city's Juvenile Employment Exchange in monitoring the progress into work of school leavers from Every Street, Chester Street, and All Souls' schools. For those not successful in finding work, a Pilgrim Boys' Club provided classes in technical skills and office training, visited unemployed lads, and organised P.T. and sport sessions. Such schemes had their successors in the more immediate past, when, by 1980, the Settlement possessed one of the leading units in the country for tackling the problem of teenage illiteracy.

The Settlement's chief draw for young people, however, was the less demanding Saturday night dance. "A good dance under thoroughly wholesome conditions," as it was described in 1918 when it had an average attendance of 200 young people. From such occasions the Settlement could draw volunteers

Ancoats 18+ Group - the first to be formed in Manchester - 1948.

PEODLE

Youth club activities - fencing

for its other activities which often made no clear distinction between 'youth' and 'adult'. The intermingling of age groups was preferred to a youth ghetto, and the Executive Committee noted with satisfaction in 1952 the success of a hot pot supper at which " a lame/blind/deaf man was seen dancing a barn dance with members of the youth club". Nevertheless, the 1940's and 1950's were perhaps the decades of the youth club. One Settlement youth club member recalls walking from Clayton every evening rain or shine to attend until his call-up in 1947. Snooker, chess and table tennis were staple activities with discussions in a room upstairs and dances on the Round House's famous maplewood floor. There were outings to Blackpool and camps at Ludworth. He was not aware of the other activities of the Settlement, nor of its history and aims. Religion

Sitting this one out! - Youth club social - 1960s.

and politics were not discussed. The aim was to have a good time.

Kathleen Kidd, wife of one of the wardens in that era, recalls from a different viewpoint the work the Settlement did to help young people in their transition to the adult world of work.

"In the Teddy Boy era we had some awful problems with the youth. They would wear these clothes and they paid an awful lot for these clothes. If they went for a job in these clothes, that was enough. The employer wouldn't look at them. So we kept trousers that were the proper width at the bottom - conventional grey flannels and sports jackets and we'd say, "if you're going for a job come in and we'll kit you out." I remember we had a man down from the employment exchange and he looked at these boys and said "You know why you can't get a job? It's because you're dressed the way you

are." He looked at one boy who was wearing a black shirt and said, "You'll never get a job in a black shirt." I thought, well really! It's all right a white shirt but how difficult to keep white shirts clean. No facilities for washing - no washing machines or anything like that." (Kathleen Kidd).

When camping holidays in Marple or North Wales began to seem tame to a more sophisticated generation of young people after World War II, Mrs. Kidd's husband, Gordon, provided more ambitious challenges. He got the Settlement to purchase a bus and began excursions on the Continent.

"We varied the groups we took abroad each year. One year I took a Monk's bus - they lent us a bus. The two of us went to Switzerland, Gordon with a group of adults and I took the youth club in a Monk's bus. The second bus cost £250 and was a Leyland bus. This was

taken to Finland and crossed the Arctic Circle. Helsinki newspaper reporters met the bus at the Arctic Circle and said they were the first British tourists in a bus to go there. Mr. Kidd was very anxious that the young man pictured by his side in the photo in front of the bus should get his HGV licence and encouraged him to drive the bus." (Kathleen Kidd).

Children and young people do not always respond appreciatively to efforts made on their behalf. Early Settlement reports contain frequent mention of uncivilised behaviour. In 1931, measures had to be taken to stop children lighting fires under the Recreation Hall, and a boundary wall collapsed under the weight of "mischievous children". In 1956, the Warden reported problems with rival gangs of children and, more worryingly, remarked that "there are signs of a colour problem."

Youth club camp site and campers (below) - Penmaenmawr, North Wales. - 1965

When this picture was taken at Abelboden, Switzerland. six journeys abroad in the Settlement bus had been safely undertaken.

"I realised that there was a group of kids that were always getting thrown out of everywhere - the Lynch's and the Twigg's who mainly lived on Hadrian's Avenue. You mentioned Hadrian's Avenue and everyone shuddered - "Oh God!". So we decided to work with them and do what we planned. So we carried on. We worked with small groups. We took them away to Ludworth Hut at Marple. That was still going then." (Eric Youd).

When the Moss Lane house opened in 1971, it aimed both to act as a focal point for children and young people in the community and to build bridges between groups in an area of mixed race. Like its Ancoats parent, it was to provide for the main needs of children which were identified as creative encouragement and contact with adults. In 1947, the Settlement's youth leader at Ancoats Mr. Hazlitt, had laid a statement of his aims and philosophy before the Executive Committee.

"We should aim at broadening and enriching the individuality of all those under our influence, and,

From Ancoats to the Artic Circle - the second Settlement bus with Gordon Kidd and driver.

though differences of approach and technique were necessary in dealing with each type and age group, in general the widest possible degree of tolerance SHORT OF ACCEPTANCE OF VIOLENCE should be practised."

A later Settlement youth worker, Eric Youd, liked to define his work, "as allowing young people the opportunity to do anything legal that they want to do."

Even in 1947, the Executive Committee found Mr. Hazlitt's statement "almost unexceptionable," although they were concerned that leaving too open a choice to young club members might "bring little call for anything beyond various forms of communal recreation." The Settlement should aim higher. Nevertheless, they "noted with satisfaction," the youth leaders promise "to encourage the young people to pass on into adult activities, present or projected." Children and young people were part of a whole, and not a distinct "juvenile problem."

c. Mothers

"I used to work a lot with families when I first came, giving them general support and advice. There was no advice centre then so a lot would be on housing benefits or grants. I'd go out and see what they needed and help them with their shopping so it was very family based work. They learned where to get help through the children coming." (Marie Williamson).

Like Jane Addams in the Chicago of the 1890's, Marie Williamson in the Manchester of the 1970's found other members of the family attracted to the Settlement through the medium of their children who were always the first to break the ice and step through the doors of Ancoats Hall, the Round House or Aidans. Mothers with infants or young children were prominent here. In the 1890's, "nursing mothers" like "young people" were being identified as a social problem by governments and by voluntary

A Tuesday At Home - mothers, children and the occasional father. - 1937

MANCHESTER ART MUSEUM AND UNIVERSITY SETTLEMENT,
ANCOATS HALL, EVERY STREET.

A Sale of Bulbs

(HYACINTHS, TULIPS, DAFFODILS, CROCUSES, &c.)

On SATURDAY, 24th Oct., 1908, from 2 to 5-0 p.m.,

AND DURING THE FOLLOWING WEEK,

Oct. 26 to Oct. 31, from 7-30 to 9-0 p.m.

HYACINTHS, various, in pot	**4d.**
TULIPS, various, three in a pot	**3d.**
CROCUSES, various, six in a pot	**2d.**
DAFFODILS, three in a pot	**3d.**
NARCISSI, five in a pot	**3d.**

On SATURDAY March 27th, 1909.

AN EXHIBITION OF

Plants Grown from the Bulbs

WILL BE HELD IN

THE ART MUSEUM, from 3 to 6-30 p.m.

Plants with owner's name attached, must be brought to the Art Museum NOT LATER than TWO o'clock p.m. on day of show, Saturday, March 27th, and must remain until close of show. The competition will be confined to residents within one mile of the Museum.

PRIZES WILL BE GIVEN FOR THE BEST SPECIMENS SHOWN.

HINTS ON GROWING BULBS.

After planting the bulbs, water the pot thoroughly and leave it until the water has drained away. Then place the pot in a cellar, backyard, or cool, dark place, and cover to about four inches above the rim with sand or fine ashes and leave it for about five weeks. Then uncover it at the top and, if the soil appear to be dry, water it and cover up again, and leave for a few weeks longer. At the end of about twelve weeks uncover again, and if the leaves are seen about one inch above the top of the bulb, take the pot out of the sand or ashes and bring it into the light; but do not expose to a strong light too suddenly.

A slender stick may be put into the pot to tie the flowering stem to. Turn the pot round occasionally, so as to ensure a straight growth of the stem.

Grow the plant slowly in a cool room, and keep as free as possible from dust or gas. The plant needs plenty of light.

The William Morris Press, 8, Lloyd Street, Deansgate, Manchester.

organisations. High infant death rates and the poor physical condition of children in inner city areas like Ancoats brought concern as to the future of the nation. By 1898, At Homes were being held at Ancoats Hall for women from the Pollard Street and Oldham Road districts. The "stiff, straight, silent rows" of the first meetings began to give way to "chatty, cosy groups of friends." In 1900, a Mothers' Meeting organised by the Ladies Public Health Society met at the Settlement, its aim being to "get the women of the neighbourhood to take a greater and more intelligent interest in their work as mothers, nurses, homemakers and citizens." Lectures on hygiene, sanitation, cookery and laundry work by health visitors and others were relieved by sing-songs and sales of bulbs and plants to brighten the back yards of Ancoats. A steady improvement in the punctuality and regularity of attendance of the 80 to 100 members was noted with approval in 1902. 40 years later, when war disrupted Settlement activities, the Mothers' Club survived. Its members often travelled in from their new estate homes for weekly meetings at the Round House. The war over, it continued to provide welcome relief for the mothers of Ancoats, many of whom had no occupation outside the household.

"The mothers have a more than full time job looking after the innumerable children for practically every family is a large one. They have little time to care for themselves and most of their money is spent on feeding and clothing the children. Occasionally they have a night out with father at the pub or the cinema, but not very often. About twenty belong to the Mothers' Club and those who have children below school age can leave them in the care of one of the girls whilst their meeting is in progress", wrote a young settlement resident in an essay for his University Social Administration course.

Brightening up Ancoats - a sale of bulbs at the Settlement.

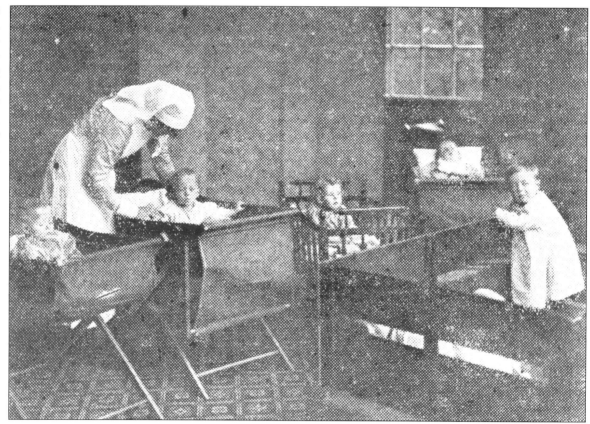

Not only could young children be cared for at Every Street, but also bathed there.

"There was no baths. For all the children to have a bath we used to have to go into a place called the University Settlement at Every Street and every week, there was a great big bath there and the bath would accommodate six children - it was that big - in one go. Boys and girls alike - it was only kids like, so sex didn't come into it. And all the mothers would bath each child in the same water. Then they'd let that water go out, put fresh water in and six more children would get in." (Mr. Lawlor).

More formal advice on family and other problems came initially through a Poor Man's Lawyer scheme, established in the Settlement in 1898. Staffed by local solicitors and law students who gave their time

Pre-school playgroup with mums - 1970.

"Then of course there was Mayfield House. It was partly accommodation for homeless families. At one time there were about 120 children living there. The mothers were allowed to go with the children into Mayfield House. There were all the old people there both women and men along with the young families. Some people had seven children. All they had was a bed, a chest of drawers at the side and their luggage was put underneath. They had trestle tables where they ate their meals. The husbands were allowed in I think between 7 p.m. and 8 p.m. most nights. They were supposed to go and find lodgings in the district. We decided to do something about it. I think it was when one of the staff was ill there and we started a playcentre there - we somehow managed to get in. Then Gordon said we ought to try something else to get these families housed so we took two flats that the Corporation lent us in Goulden Street. We gradually moved the mothers out from Mayfield House to Goulden so they realised that they could use sub standard accommodation like this for

and advice free of charge, its case load rapidly increased from 50 consultations in its first year to over 500 by 1902. Husband/wife disputes accounted for a high proportion of the problems advised on, with tenant/landlord and employee/employer disputes running close behind. Its role was later to be taken on by the Citizens' Advice Bureau or by Welfare Rights Centres such as that opened in Heatherbank House in 1975, staffed by Mr. Burslem and volunteers from Manchester Polytechnic's Department of Law and Social Science.

Practical help as well as advice was offered to families in distress.

Keep fit class - 1936

PEOPLE

Beswick Women's Health Project - 1990.

centre." (Jacky Horner).

Helping as well as being helped was central to the Settlement's tradition. Mothers who attended it were far from being passive recipients of help and advice. In 1919, they formed an active Ancoats branch of Manchester's Womens' Citizen Association, organising socials and dances, providing the cast of plays and always ready to help in countless ways. "I believe it is because we are the friends and neighbours of our women. We touch the family at every point" wrote the Warden, Beatrice Rogers.

families instead of housing them as we did. (Kathleen Kidd).

"We were given so many hours to get out of Guernsey and we were going to go to this Mayfield House. When I got back from Guernsey my auntie said, "No, no we'll try and put you up". She managed to get us a one up one down in Woodward Street, off Buckler Street so we managed to get a place and didn't have to go in. Then when I got involved with the Round House and got to an age when you wanted to help because you'd been helped, we went in with paints and toys and tried to help the children who were not occupied, you know, the children who were just put out. That was the idea, getting us to go in and help and take equipment. So there was what looked like a proper bed for the mums and then three smaller ones and the cots down the

"Women were coming in saying that they had needs in different areas, health wise and relating those to Helen (Reeve) and Pat (Williams). What later happened was that they had their own room and a drop in so there was the informal work and this area here became the women's base so women could come in and access Pat, who became the women's health worker, and discuss any problems they may have with Pat and then we could look at formalising that into some sessions." (Marie Williamson).

The language of the 1980's contrasts with that of 1918 but the feeling of a democratic two way relationship remains in the Settlement's contacts with its women neighbours.

d. Old people

The elderly were not prominent amongst the neighbours of the first Settlement residents in Every Street. As better living standards and falling mortality brought increasing expectations of a longer life in the twentieth century, so old people came to be recognised as a group with social needs. In 1946, the Annual Report recorded as a new venture the formation of an over-60's club to meet on Tuesday and Friday afternoons.

"So we started dinners for them." Over 60's lunch club. - 1970

"Jean and I started an Old People's Club in 1949. I had been to Toynbee (Hall) and seen an Old People's Club there and I thought that one day, I'm going to have an Old People's Club. So that's one of the things we started. Following on from that the local doctors were saying that there was an awful lot of malnutrition among the elderly and they felt that if they had a good meal a week, this might push them above the position where they were malnourished. So we started dinners for them. I think we were the first to do this." (Kathleen Kidd).

"We used to do the Christmas dinner me and her (Mrs. Kirkman), me and her and another lady called Lily Lee. She was a friend and we used to cook their (Over 60's) Christmas dinner down in the cellar. We had a proper kitchen, you know. For 200 for Christmas dinner. Turkey, carrots, peas, roast potatoes and one year we got from Australia a great big Christmas pudding in a round bowl like that." (Flo Beddows).

"200 for Christmas dinner." Over 60's Christmas party. - 1980

Care of the aged did not end with the provision of dinners and later of a chiropody service. As with the young, getting them out of Ancoats on an outing

PEOPLE

or a holiday was thought to be important.

"*A unique feature of my Settlement years was Pensioners' Week at the Summer Camp with the provision of beds, bedding and additional heating, and on chilly evenings, old people lining up to have their hot water bottles filled. Nor were the pensioners slow to show their appreciation. For when the helpers did the rounds at bed time, there were many offers of alcoholic refreshment.*" (Clive Johnston).

Other holidays were organised for the elderly in the more conventional surroundings of a boarding house or private hotel, as well as at

Gwyrych Castle in North Wales arranged by Julia Dobrashian and described by one helper as a "kind of upmarket Butlins."

Senior Settlement Member - Mrs Johnson, aged 90, 1970s

Like other settlement neighbours, old people were not seen as passive recipients of goodwill.

"They opened a workshop downstairs (1968) for old people. Just a couple of hours in the morning and another lot would do a couple of hours in the afternoon. They used to get 15 shilling a week. You know these fairy lights, well the bulbs, they'd put them in boxes, fill them up. Well I used to take them cups of tea in, take a big tea pot down, pour them a cup of tea out. Not only just that but that's one of the jobs that used to be done." (Flo Beddows).

More conventional pensioners' holidays - sunny Rhyl 1953.

PEOPLE

A Settlement response to an increasing problem. - Leaflet issued in 1932.

e. The Unemployed

Some of those senior citizens in the Round House workshop might well, as younger men and women, have experienced the hardships of unemployment which beset Ancoats as it did other industrial areas in the 1920's and 1930's. Solutions for this problem were beyond the powers of governments, let along the settlement, but Manchester University Settlement used its experience of creative organisation to provide relief from the monotony of long term joblessness. "The burden of unemployment", wrote the Warden,

Richard Heath - Pilgrim club founder and leader.

MANCHESTER UNIVERSITY SETTLEMENT.

DAY CLUBS *for* MEN *and* BOYS.

An Experiment and an Appeal for Volunteers.

October, 1932.

Hilda Cashmore, in her annual report of 1929, "and its retinue of ills, both spiritual and physical, make our work ever more necessary and more anxious. We do not wish to give relief. We think that to trifle with inadequate schemes of this sort would spoil our relations with a courageous and independent people and would do no good."

Instead of relief, a club for unemployed men and boys was founded in 1931, and named the Pilgrim Club to commemorate the fact that its origin lay in a grant of £500 from a national charity, the Pilgrim Trust.

"Dad was wandering round out of work for four years on and off. The Pilgrim Club started and Lady

Visit of the Duke of Kent to an unemployed men's club. Richard Heath to right of picture.

Mabel (Smith) knew dad because dad was church warden at St. Edwards (?) and knew that he was used to welfare because he had been a shop steward. Lady Mabel said 'We do need a leader', so he started to go then. Dad was just dedicated. I think he got paid 39/- a week for running the Pilgrim Club. It was full time because unemployment was in such a state that the Lord Mayor set up clubs all over Manchester and the Pilgrim Club was twinned to one in Hulme". (Stanley Heath).

Open from Monday to Friday with a membership of 200 and an average daily attendance of 70, its

*Field of Dreams -
Pilgrim Club
Baseball Team 1935.*

activities were decided upon by a committee elected by the membership. A 2d per week membership fee ensured that it was not a charity. Occupations such as shoe repairing, general repairs and carpentry were provided in the morning. Football and baseball teams played in the afternoon with a flourishing allotments group for those who preferred a different type of outdoor activity.

"Dad organised the football. All the clubs in the scheme took part in the Lord Mayor's Cup. The final was

at Maine Road. The Duke of York was to present the trophy. Dad introduced him to the teams. He wondered because one of the settlement team stuttered. So did the Duke of York, and he thought, "What's going to happen when they get to him and he says something to him?" Anyway a newsreader was there and when they got to him they cut it out. However, he didn't stutter at all and neither did the Duke of York but they cut it out of the newsreel. The Settlement won the cup of course. We had a baseball team. There were men who came along to the Pilgrim Club. Wilfred Pickles, also out of work, used to come along and entertain the men and Violet Carson. That's what kept them going until things improved." (Stanley Heath).

Joan Seaton remembers her father, Charles Seaton, himself unemployed, acting as cook for the canteen which the Club's members organised to provide cheap dinners at 2d and 1d for children.

"He was a master baker by trade. It was voluntary work. None of them were paid. I was brought up on Every Street just opposite the Round House, well just a little way along. The meals he made was a main dinner and always a pan of stew for them who didn't want the meat and veg. There was meat, two veg and potatoes. For that they paid two pence in old money. Then there was always a set pudding and then always rice pudding because I always had the skin off the rice pudding. He cooked for all the poor people of the area." (Joan Seaton).

In addition to organising these activities, the Pilgrim Club's leader, Richard Heath, advised upon many of the legal and bureaucratic problems which arose for the unemployed. The annual report for 1934/5 noted that the club leader had been involved in a good deal of hard work on behalf of his members as a result of the new unemployment assistance scheme introduced by the Unemployment Act of 1934. Not all his problems were of this nature.

"There was one particular street where the workhouse was. Just as you were coming to the bottom between the Round House and Ancoats Hall. There was a street off

there. The police were there. There had to be two to go down there. One day, one of the chaps down there - a policeman went into his house and came out with a big black eye. He hadn't got a warrant. He came into the Settlement and said to Dad 'I've got court tomorrow'. He said 'He came after me, down the street followed me into the house without a warrant and so I gave him a black eye'. So my dad had to go to Mitchell Street and when the magistrate heard it he said that he didn't have a warrant and he went in an area where there should have been two police and he said it was his own fault." (Stanley Heath).

Richard Heath established a close working relationship with his members which other Settlement workers, including the Warden, Rendell Wyatt, found it hard to emulate.

"My dad went out to do some work at Edale and left Mr Wyatt at the Settlement. They used a famous word there beginning with "b". My dad said, 'Don't say that to any of these men, while I'm away, Rendell'. He did. He had a black eye when dad got back. One of the unemployed had thumped him one." (Stanley Heath).

Richard Heath resigned in 1944 to take a post as welfare officer for the Port of Manchester Rehabilitation Committee. Total war had proved to be the swiftest solution to the unemployment problem and the Pilgrim Club no longer had a purpose. Its work, however, had brought the Settlement into contact with adult males, normally the group least attracted by settlement activities.

f. Actors

One activity in which Pilgrim Club members, along with other Settlement residents and neighbours, did involve themselves was that of drama. From its origins in the Ancoats Art Museum, the Settlement was always heavily involved in the creative arts. An impressive programme of lectures and concerts fills the early annual reports. Even by 1944, it was noted, rather sadly, that a lecture on the "Uses of Poetry" in the Ancoats Sunday Evening Lecture series had been poorly attended. Such passive absorption of culture, however, clashed with the Settlement ideal of participation in activities which would bring residents and neighbours together. Music and the drama were of central importance here as Jacky Homer's reluctant involvement in the choir, and Malcolm Lynch's boys in the Nativity play have already shown.

The early annual reports record not only lectures and classes but the Art Museum Choral Society, the Amateur Dramatic Society and the Ancoats Elizabethan Society, founded by Eva Gore-Booth, which performed The Merchant of Venice in June 1899. Such activities continued to be a leading feature of Settlement life, reaching their peak, perhaps, in the 1930's, when the Settlement Players staged regular productions and caught the critical eye of the Manchester Guardian.

"An unusual and attractive performance was given at the Round House, Every Street, Manchester last night

MANCHESTER
Art Museum and University Settlemer

Ancoats Hall, Every Street.

WINTER PROGRAMME, 1905-6.

The Art Museum is Open to Visitors every week-day (except Tuesday) from 1 to 5 and 7 to 9.3
On Sundays it is Open from 2 to 5.

Classes and Lectures will be held as under :—

HISTORY CLASS (chiefly for the study of Current Events) will meet on alt
Mondays, beginning 16th October. Leader : A. D. Lindsay, M.A.

NATURE STUDY CLASS (for the study of Plant Life) will meet on alt
Tuesdays, beginning 17th October. Leader : Miss Marie Stopes, D. Sc. F

NATURE OBSERVATION CLASS (for the cultivation of power of obser
by drawing natural objects, chiefly plants) on alternate Tuesdays, beg
24th October. Leader : H. J. Mapleton.

LITERATURE CLASS (for the reading and study of good books) on alt
Wednesdays, beginning 18th October. Leader :

ENGLISH COMPOSITION CLASS will meet on alternate Wedne
beginning on 25th October.

MATTER AND MOTION : An INTRODUCTION TO PHYSICAL SCIENCE
general title of a series of talks to be given on alternate Mondays, begi
23rd October, by Herbert Stansfield, B.Sc. A.I.E.E.

Recreation :—

POPULAR CONCERTS, weekly, on Mondays at 8 p.m., beginning 23rd Oct
"AT HOMES," weekly, on Tuesdays from 7.30 to 10 p.m.
CHILDREN'S ENTERTAINMENTS, weekly, on Fridays at 7 p.m.
DANCES in Recreation Rooms, weekly, on Saturdays from 7.30 to 10.30
Admission—Men, 6d.; Women, 4d.

Clubs and Societies :—

LITTLE GIRLS' CLUB—Monday, Tuesday and Wednesday.
SENIOR GIRLS' CLUB—Tuesday, Wednesday and Thursday.
GROSVENOR ST. GIRLS' & BOYS' CLUB—Every week-night, except
JERSEY ST. LADS' CLUB—Every week-night.
CHORAL SOCIETY. Hon. Conductor, Mr. H. A. Minton. Hon. Sec.,
E. J. Minton.
MANCHESTER GLEEMEN (Male Voice Choir). Hon. Conductor, Mr.
Minton. Hon. Sec., Mr. Lees.

These Societies will hold joint meetings beginning at 7.15 p.m. on 3rd
for the study of Handel's " Messiah."

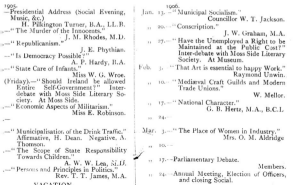

and Societies *(continued).*

25

RPHEUS ORCHESTRAL SOCIETY meets weekly on Tuesdays at 8 p.m. Hon. Conductor, Mr. H. J. Dunckley. Hon. Sec., Mr. C. Cooling.

MATEUR DRAMATIC SOCIETY meets weekly on Mondays at 8 p.m. Hon. Secretary, Mr. J. E. Chatfield.

ELD CLUB meets after Nature Study Classes on Tuesdays. Hon. Sec., Mr. W. T. Watson.

AWCETT DEBATING SOCIETY (for Women) meets weekly on Wednesdays at 8 p.m. Hon. Pres., Miss Crompton. Hon. Secs., Mrs. Burke and Mrs. Brierley.

OTHERS' MEETING meets weekly on Thursdays at 3 p.m. Hon. Superintendent, Mrs. Rigby Armitage.

OYNBEE DEBATING SOCIETY (for Men and Women) meets weekly on Saturdays at 7.30 p.m. Hon. President, H. Pilkington Turner, B.A., LL.B. Hon. Secretary and Treasurer, J. W. Bagnall. Co-Secretary, W. Hallows.

SYLLABUS 1905-6.

1905.

—Presidential Address (Social Evening, Music, &c.)
  H. Pilkington Turner, B.A., LL.B.
—"The Murder of the Innocents."
  J. M. Rhodes, M.D.
—"Republicanism."
  J. E. Phythian.
—"Is Democracy Possible?"
  A. P. Hardy, B.A.
—"State Care of Infants."
  Miss W. G. Wroe.
(Friday).—"Should Ireland be allowed Entire Self-Government?" Inter-debate with Moss Side Literary Society. At Moss Side.
—"Economic Aspects of Militarism."
  Miss E. Robinson.
—
—"Municipalisation of the Drink Traffic." Affirmative, H. Dean. Negative, A. Thomson.
—"The Scope of State Responsibility Towards Children."
  A. W. W. Lea, M.D.
—"Persons and Principles in Politics."
  Rev. T. T. James, M.A.
  VACATION.

1906.

Jan. 13.—"Municipal Socialism."
  Councillor W. T. Jackson.
  „ 20.—"Conscription."
  J. W. Graham, M.A.
  „ 27.—"Have the Unemployed a Right to be Maintained at the Public Cost?" Inter-debate with Moss Side Literary Society. At Museum.
Feb. 3.—"That Art is essential to happy Work."
  Raymond Unwin.
  „ 10.—"Mediæval Craft Guilds and Modern Trade Unions."
  W. Mellor.
  „ 17.—"National Character."
  G. B. Hertz, M.A., B.C.L.
  „ 24.—
Mar. 3.—"The Place of Women in Industry."
  Mrs. O. M. Aldridge.
  „ 10.—
  „ 17.—Parliamentary Debate.
  Members.
  „ 24.—Annual Meeting, Election of Officers, and closing Social.

ding **Parties for the Blind** are held weekly on Mondays at 3 p.m.

• **Santa Fina Branch** cares for the physically disabled in the district. Hon. Sec., Miss Helen Fisher.

• **Poor Man's Lawyer** gives gratuitous legal advice to those unable to obtain it in the ordinary way on Mondays at 7 p.m.

• **Associates** comprise those who give personal service in Settlement activities. They will welcome new members. The Associates have a library, and carry on a country cottage. They hold meetings on the first Friday in each month, and Associate visitors meet on the third Friday in each month at 8 p.m. Hon. secretaries, J. J. Mallon and Dolly Parker.

• **Wardens** are always glad to give further information. Their office hours (at the Art Museum) are from 11 to 12.30 and 7 to 9.30 daily.—Alice Crompton, T. R. Marr, Wardens.

when the Settlement Players presented Purcell's opera 'The Fairy Queen' with words from 'A Midsummer Night's Dream'. The effect was as might be expected to enhance the unreality of Shakespeare's work and to make the dream more fantastic and far more colourful than it has ever previously appeared. The result was not a synthesis and not in any sense a unified work of art but it was a rich and splendid and at times beautiful medley of poetry, charming music, dances and fine dresses." (Manchester Guardian May 30th 1935).

Cultural Ambitions - Settlement Winter Programme for 1905-06

Concert Advertisement c.1905

Concert advertisement and ticket - 1905

Productions were of an ambitious nature. The works of Shakespeare vied with those of contemporary playwrights. One of these, John Masefield's <u>Trial of Jesus</u> brought problems with the censor in 1938 because of the depiction of Christ by an actor. Two plays, <u>Everyman of Every Street</u>, and <u>Dr. Scholefield</u> were written specially for the Settlement Players by Mary Stocks, the Settlement's historian and wife of Professor J. L. Stocks, Vice Chairman of the Settlement Council. <u>Dr. Scholefield</u>, based on an imaginary episode in the life of the builder of the Round Chapel in Every Street, was first produced for the Settlement's Golden Jubilee celebrations in 1945.

Neighbours, residents and other workers all took part in these productions, at least according to the <u>Manchester Guardian</u>.

"The cast for <u>Much Ado About Nothing</u> will include unemployed men, students and business and professional people who help in the Settlement's work. Mr. Oscar Hudes has arranged among other pieces an old French Pavane, "Belle qui tiens ma vie" for a string quartet and Miss Edna Farber has through researches into the history of the dance, reconstructed a pavane and a galliard to be danced by the player". (<u>Manchester Guardian</u> March 23rd 1939).

Stanley Heath has somewhat different impressions.

"There was a religious play. The only time I ever saw it using three stages. Two side stages and a centre stage. There were some local people in the production - in the crowd scenes! They didn't get the plum parts. The Pilgrim Club built the scenery in the workshop." (Stanley Heath).

Manchester Art Museum & University Settlement

Ancoats Hall,
Every Street, Ancoats.

A GRAND CONCERT
══════ SMOKING PERMITTED ══════

WILL BE HELD IN THE RECREATION ROOMS, 20, EVERY STREET, ON THURSDAY, OCT. 26, 1905, AT EIGHT P.M.

NO CHILDREN admitted ❧ ❧ This Programme admits the **BEARER** and a **FRIEND**.

Manchester Art Museum & University Settlement.   1915

A Grand Concert

(SMOKING PERMITTED) ❧ WILL BE HELD IN THE RECREATION ROOMS, 20, EVERY ST., ANCOATS, ON THURSDAY, 23RD NOVEMBER, AT EIGHT P.M. ❧ BRIGHT MUSIC ❧ REFRESHMENTS AT LOW PRICES.

NO CHILDREN.   This Ticket admits
                                    BEARER & FRIEND.

The Settlement players - Purcell's Fairy Queen, produced in 1935.

Whether as spear carriers, principals or spectators, many of the productions were appreciated by neighbours.

"*Cinderella up to date was one of the productions that I absolutely loved. Cinderella up to date was the story of Cinderella but Prince Charming was an airforce officer. I can remember that he was very handsome in his airforce uniform. After the play had been on - it was on for about three or four nights, I think, there was a notice in the glass noticeboard outside "Lost! One R.A.F. uniform. Finder please contact."* (Joan Seaton).

Dramatic activity spread from Ancoats with its excellent facilities in the Round House to Gorton

Drama production 1905 - The New Islington Public Hall was the meeting place of Charles Rowley's Ancoats Brotherhood.

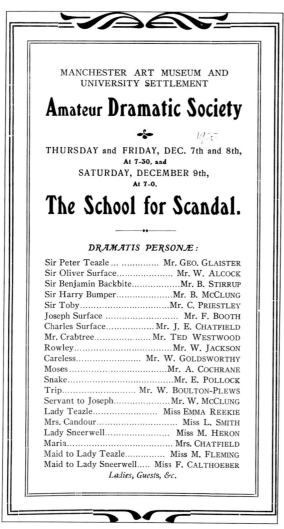

MANCHESTER ART MUSEUM AND UNIVERSITY SETTLEMENT

Amateur Dramatic Society

THURSDAY and FRIDAY, DEC. 7th and 8th,
At 7-30, and
SATURDAY, DECEMBER 9th,
At 7-0,

The School for Scandal.

DRAMATIS PERSONÆ:

Sir Peter Teazle ... . Mr. GEO. GLAISTER
Sir Oliver Surface.................... Mr. W. ALCOCK
Sir Benjamin Backbite..................Mr. B. STIRRUP
Sir Harry Bumper....................Mr. B. McCLUNG
Sir Toby................................Mr. C. PRIESTLEY
Joseph Surface .... Mr. F. BOOTH
Charles Surface.................. Mr. J. E. CHATFIELD
Mr. Crabtree.................... Mr. TED WESTWOOD
Rowley................................Mr. W. JACKSON
Careless...................... Mr. W. GOLDSWORTHY
Moses.....................................Mr. A. COCHRANE
Snake.................................Mr. E. POLLOCK
Trip.......................... Mr. W. BOULTON-PLEWS
Servant to Joseph...................Mr. W. McCLUNG
Lady Teazle....................... Miss EMMA REEKIE
Mrs. Candour........................... Miss L. SMITH
Lady Sneerwell...................... Miss M. HERON
Maria.................................... Mrs. CHATFIELD
Maid to Lady Teazle.............. Miss M. FLEMING
Maid to Lady Sneerwell..... Miss F. CALTHOEBER
Ladies, Guests, &c.

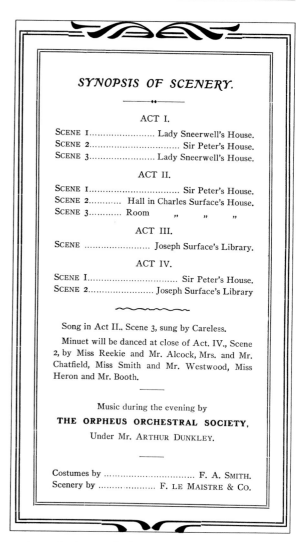

SYNOPSIS OF SCENERY.

ACT I.
SCENE 1......................... Lady Sneerwell's House.
SCENE 2............................... Sir Peter's House.
SCENE 3....................... Lady Sneerwell's House.

ACT II.
SCENE 1................................ Sir Peter's House.
SCENE 2........... Hall in Charles Surface's House.
SCENE 3........... Room   „   „   „

ACT III.
SCENE .... Joseph Surface's Library.

ACT IV.
SCENE 1................................. Sir Peter's House.
SCENE 2....................... Joseph Surface's Library.

Song in Act II., Scene 3, sung by Careless.

Minuet will be danced at close of Act. IV., Scene 2, by Miss Reekie and Mr. Alcock, Mrs. and Mr. Chatfield, Miss Smith and Mr. Westwood, Miss Heron and Mr. Booth.

Music during the evening by

THE ORPHEUS ORCHESTRAL SOCIETY,

Under Mr. ARTHUR DUNKLEY.

Costumes by .... F. A. SMITH.
Scenery by .... F. LE MAISTRE & CO.

where <u>Aladdin</u> was staged with great success early in 1945. A few months later, a project was launched to draw together different age groups in a dramatic society. Acting and singing supported Settlement aims of cultural enlightenment and of active shared participation.

Masefield's Trial of Jesus which caused problems of censorship in 1938.

Settlement Players' production of Mary Stocks' Dr. Scholefield (1934) which dramatised an incident in the life of the founder of the Round Chapel (later the Round House).

Guy Kendall - 1901

g. Wardens and Directors

For all its insistence on active and equal participation by neighbours in its activities, Settlement programmes could not have been devised and developed without its workers, whether resident in the Settlement houses or not. At the head of activity was the Warden or Director as he/she came to be called when the rather archaic Oxbridge term was given up in favour of something more in keeping with late 20th century professionalism. In 1895, two wardens were appointed. Miss Stoehr, headed the women's residence and E. T. Campagnac, the men's. Both resigned in 1898, the Annual Report of that year hoping that "they find new spheres of work amid less trying

Alice Crompton - 1900

J. Howard Whitehouse - 1909 (right)

*Sheila S. McKay
- 1940*

*Hilda Cashmore
- 1926/1931 (left)*

*H. Gordon Kidd
- 1949*

*Ralph E. Reedman
- 1946 (left)*

PEOPLE

surroundings." Ancoats had taken an early toll. Alice Crompton, a graduate of Owens College, succeeded Miss Stoehr, and with the appointment of T. R. "Citizen" Marr as men's warden in 1902, there began what the Settlement's historian has called its "golden age".

"But if they moved slowly, the reformers of those years at any rate moved forward - and with no thought of ever having to move back. They built without fear of destruction. The problems they encountered were big enough to awe and stimulate them, but not so big as to overcome them and belittle their varied tasks of personal service, experiment and analysis. Those were indeed good years for social workers." (Mary Stocks, <u>Fifty Years in Every Street</u> 1945 p.24).

Crompton and Marr resigned together in 1909,

as the brilliant team of younger workers they had drawn to Ancoats began to disperse to positions elsewhere. In their place, the Settlement Council appointed only one Warden, first male in the persons of J. H. Whitehouse, from Toynbee Hall, followed in 1911 by G. V. Cox, who also had London settlement experience at Mansfield House, and by G. K. Grierson, formerly secretary of the Salford League of Help, then female with Beatrice Rogers in 1917 followed by Hilda Cashmore in 1926. On Cashmore's resignation in 1933, the Settlement appointed a married couple Rendell and Jean Wyatt, as joint wardens. This experiment was not repeated when the Wyatts went their separate ways in 1940, although the immediate post war period saw Wardens like Ralph Reedman and Gordon Kidd bring wives and families into settlement residences.

In an institution as diverse and broadly conceived as a settlement, the role of its head is no easy one. Its pioneering mission demands a constant search for new ideas and schemes of work. At the same time, existing organisations have to be kept active. Workers, some of them until recent times residents, have to be appointed and supervised. The neighbours, whether in Ancoats, Gorton, Moss Side or Beswick have to be lived with, and helped without hint of patronage when they drop in with their problems. Business and professional people including academics on settlement council and executive committee have to be listened to, and their ideas, where possible,implemented. Some wardens were themselves academics faced with the

Cooking dinner in Switzerland - Gordon Kidd, warden 1948 - 1959, and Mrs. Kirkman.

challenges of research, publication and supervision of resident students. Above all, the ever nagging question of fund raising, budget balancing and the maintenance of ageing physical plant had to be kept in mind. Salaries were minimal and accommodation especially for a family, inconvenient. The Warden's/Director's role, that of a secular vicar, is not an easy one to play, and thus, not surprisingly, Manchester has had 20 wardens/directors in the first century of its history.

Those who stayed longest were inevitably the best remembered with the other worldly Beatrice Rogers, the dynamic Hilda Cashmore and her assistant, the socialist aristocrat, Lady Mabel Smith, and the practical visionary Gordon Kidd recreating in their terms of office something of the "golden age" which Crompton and Marr had inspired in the early years.

PEOPLE

h. Residents

Tariff for residents - 1908

Wardens and their families were not of course the only settlement personnel to take up residence in Ancoats. Settlements on the lines that Samuel Barnett had conceived were to be residential. Socially concerned people were to live in the settlement house and experience directly the environmental and other problems facing their poor neighbours in the community. Manchester University Settlement's first constitution gave the warden power to admit residents for a three month trial period, after which they might be elected to permanent status by a committee of settlement workers. The first Annual Report shows one female resident, Miss Meta Gray, sharing 114, Higher Ardwick Street with the women's warden Miss Stoehr, and four male residents living at 17, Manor Street, Ardwick with the men's warden E. T. Campagnac. Unless appointed to a salaried worker's post which included board and lodging, residents paid for their meals and accommodation. In 1902, male residents paid 21 shillings a week, or 15 shillings if lunch and tea were not taken during the week. Women also paid 21 shillings, although 31 shillings and 6d was charged to those who required a private sitting room. Fires in private rooms were charged for. The concessionary rate for men implies that they might be out during the day in city offices, university departments or other places of employment. Women residents in 1902 were more likely to be in the settlement house or its immediate vicinity. Thus they would normally require lunch and tea during the week and also private space, whilst male residents would be content with a common room for their leisure needs. Residents, the Annual Report for 1900 explained, were not expected to give their whole time, as those in a college or university would be, to

---

THE HOUSES OF RESIDENCE

are situated, for women, at Ancoats Hall, and, for men, at 20, Every Street. Residents are admitted by the Wardens of the Men's and Women's Houses respectively. A large increase in the number of both resident and non-resident workers is needed, if the objects of the Association are to be carried out.

Tariff—Men's House.

Board and lodging, per week	£1 1 0
Ditto (exclusive of lunch and tea, Monday to Friday), per week	£0 15 0

Tariff—Women's House.

Board and lodging, per week	£1 1 0
Ditto, with private sitting-room....................	£1 11 6

Fires in private rooms are charged extra.

Visitors and Non-Resident Workers.—Visitors are admitted to the Houses from time to time for short periods, and Non-Resident Workers may make use of the Houses for occasional meals.

Tariff for Visitors and Non-Resident Workers.

	Visitors	Workers
Breakfast, Lunch, or High Tea...	£0 1 0	£0 0 9
Afternoon Tea	0 0 4	0 0 3
Dinner............................	0 1 6	0 1 0
Dinner, Bed, and Breakfast.........	0 3 6	0 3 0
Ditto, with Lunch....................	0 4 6	0 3 6
Week-end (Saturday Dinner to Monday breakfast, inclusive)...	0 6 0	0 5 0
Board and Lodging, per week ...	1 8 0	1 4 6
Ditto, with private Sitting-room	1 18 0	1 14 6

Fires in private rooms are charged extra.

the institution but were expected to take "a serious interest in its social efforts." There was no reason, it continued, to fear disastrous effects from residence at Ancoats Hall. Life there was simple "but cheerful and not devoid of those comforts which are generally regarded as necessary," comforts which included domestic staff to provide meals, cleaning and the like.

Settlement Associates' activities - 1907/08.

World War One brought a temporary end to residence, but after some re-arrangement of accommodation, a women's residence re-opened at 20, Every Street in November 1917. The 1921 Annual report records five women in residence for periods of between a month and two years between 1918 and 1921. In 1927, residents included three women from the U.S.A. and, in the following year, the six female and seven male residents included women from Toronto, Hamburg and Tokyo. Eighteen residents, eleven of them female were living at the Settlement in 1930, with three more living with Miss Jenkinson on the Wilbraham Estate. A Residents' Association was formed in the following year. With the establishment of a new Department of Social Study at the University and the appointment of Hilda Cashmore as its Supervisor of Practical Work,

in 1926, settlement residence came to be used as the base from which social work students could gain practical experience. An Oxford student, and five from Edinburgh, as well as Manchester students, were in residence in 1928, experiencing the real social problems on which to test their classroom expertise. By this time, former settlement residents were operating in a variety of social work posts. Barbara de Vitre had become a policewoman in Sheffield and Miss Isherwood, a welfare supervisor in a Shanghai cotton mill. Miss Daniels, her Manchester social studies diploma completed, had been appointed warden of the David Lewis Club, Liverpool and Miss Allison, sub-warden of its Women's Settlement in Everton. Miss Knox, with an Oxford social science diploma tested by six months residence in Ancoats,

Gorton - 1948

Group with Mr. & Mrs. Kidd - 1949

pointing out the advantages of settlement residence for members of school staff or graduate students. This may have been an attempt not only to draw residents from a broader occupational sector but also to increase the number of residents which had fallen from 18 in 1930 to 7 by 1935. It met with some success as the house was reported to be full in 1938, although the approach of war in 1939 brought "a general exodus of regular residents combined with

had become a worker for the L.C.C.'s Care Committee. Settlement residence was becoming a form of internship for the emergent profession of social work, although it was not compulsory.

"I was interviewed for the Course in Social Administration by Barbara Rodgers and she suggested that I live at the University Settlement. This was not expected or required of Social Administration students but they hoped that one or two each year would take advantage of the experience. I imagine that it was suggested in my case because of my previous involvement in youth work before joining the navy." (George Saddington).

Social work trainees did not constitute the whole body of settlement residents. In 1936, one new male resident was an almoner at the Northern Hospital and another a member of the staff of Ferrantis Ltd. At the same time, the heads of the Manchester Grammar School and Manchester High School as well as the deans of faculties in the university were written to the prospect of a number of short term ones."

Residence appears to have continued during World War II both at Ancoats and at Gorton, where full board in 1942 cost £2 a week and part board, 35 shillings. Visitors to the settlement could have a snack, bed and breakfast and a bath for 1 shilling and 6 pence with lunch or supper for 1 shilling and 3 pence and tea for six pence. Students from Edinburgh were in residence during the Easter vacation and applications for residence at Gorton had to be refused for lack of accommodation.

After 1945, despite rationing and the need to renovate ageing buildings, the executive committee confirmed its belief in residence. It stressed the desirability of club leaders at Ancoats being in residence, and remarked, rather scornfully, that a visit to Liverpool University Settlement had shown it to

Derbyshire outing - 1950

have "become little more than a residence for social science students." A special committee set up in 1948 to assess the Settlement's aims and purpose agreed that "residence was an essential part of the Settlement and that Ancoats was the place for it." George Saddington, a social administration student and resident at Ancoats Hall from 1949 - 51, confirmed this view in a course essay he wrote on "The Value of Residence in a Settlement."

In front of Ancoats Hall - 1950

"For the last six months we have lived, worked and played together with never a dull moment and never a sad one. It is wonderful to relate that such a community exists of which toleration is the greatest asset and discussion the foremost practice. In such a pleasant and sociable atmosphere of youth -for ages range from 18 to 26 - differences have been settled by discussion and much has been learned by all about each other, people, places,

Fred Marquis gained his first Settlement experience as a member of the Ancoats Associates, and later, as Lord Woolton, became chancellor of the University of Manchester - 1944

arts, sciences, religion and politics, but mainly about life itself in all its aspects." (George Saddington).

"Very interesting," commented his tutor, awarding the essay a mark of B++.

With Gordon Kidd's appointment as Warden in 1948, and his move with his family to a flat in the Round House, it was decided that Ancoats Hall with its dining room, lounge and five study bedrooms should be used entirely for residential purposes. Charges were three pounds five shillings a week, or two pounds ten shillings if a room was shared. Diet was plain, if nourishing.

"Lord and Lady Woolton also came to dinner on one occasion, although Settlement dinners were anything but lavish affairs. At one time, we had a housekeeper who would regularly dish up macaroni cheese, followed by macaroni pudding in the interest of economy. Nevertheless, we residents all got on extremely well and shared in the washing up after dinner, often singing as we did it." (George Saddington).

"I lived in the Round House and Ancoats Hall. There was a small students' residence in Ancoats Hall. At that time, there was only our wing which was occupied, the rest of it was empty. We were virtually living with no heating in the winter of '62/63 and I ran the residence. It was horrendous." (Eric Youd).

As Eric Youd indicates, problems began to emerge with settlement residence. Residents' fees had constituted an important source of revenue for Manchester as for other settlements. Numbers fell in the 1950's, and residence ceased to pay its own way let alone generate income for other activities. Although it was agreed to pay a higher rent for Ancoats Hall in 1954 because "it was vital to have a residence in the locality of the settlement," the building, particularly its heating, was creating an expense which residence fees could not offset. Residence was ceasing to be the central feature of settlement work, and was increasingly being used, where still offered, as a cheap form of student accommodation which generated some revenue. In the mid - 1960's, the central organisation of the British Settlement Movement, the British Association of Residential Settlements, decided to drop the adjective "residential" from its title. By 1970, only four American settlement houses had residence facilities. In 1963, Manchester University Settlement gave up the tenancy of Ancoats Hall whilst maintaining small residences at Starr Avenue and at St. Aidan's Rectory. In 1964, Keith Hill, who had succeeded Gordon Kidd as Warden in 1960, moved to a house in Rusholme. In 1967, the Settlement gave up the theory and practice of residence.

i. Non Resident Workers

Although the residents, full and part time, provided a core around which settlement activities could group, and to which neighbours could relate, they were always a minority of workers. Much of the thrust and activity in the early years of the Settlement came, not from the residents alone, but from a group of mainly young, and not very wealthy, people who came to Ancoats to help in settlement work. Forming themselves into a body called the Settlement Associates in 1898, and asking no financial subscription other than what each could afford, they went about doing good by enjoying themselves. They organised socials, debates and drama productions, rambled and camped in the Derbyshire hills and involved themselves in local and national political activity campaigning for women's suffrage and against sweated labour. "Residents and helpers," said the Annual Report of 1901, "live in the spirit of friends and neighbours not of teachers or patrons." By 1907, the Associates had an active membership of

J.J. Mallon, secretary of the associates in the early 1900's, pictured with his bust on retirement as Warden of Toynbee Hall - 1955.

173 and elected six representatives to the Settlement Council. The majority of members, it was claimed, came from the very people for whom the Settlement was founded.

"Mill hands, artisans and unskilled labourers work together with those who have had the advantages of better conditions and a higher education. We claim to have succeeded in doing what few other settlements have done, to have created an efficient body of helpers from the working classes of our neighbourhood." (Annual Report 1906-07).

"The atmosphere - the contact with responsive people - with warmth - with enquiring minds - social service a basic idea without the mawkish attitude met in religious circles. (I) did not find it at the Settlement - a sound,

healthy practical outlook prevailed - nobody preached or prayed at you. Two Saturday evening Toynbee debating opponents would go rambling in the same groups on the Sunday - discussing the distribution of plant life on the chalk soil of Derbyshire - or they would jointly carry cripples to the Santa Fina social or work the lemon peeling machine for the associates' evening drink. Even the friction was firmly friendly." (Theresa Billington Grieg).

The Associates' secretary, the jeweller's assistant J.J. (Jimmy) Mallon was to rise to prominence via the anti-sweating campaign of 1906 and the Whitley Committee of 1916 to become Warden of Toynbee Hall and a leading figure in the twentieth century settlement movement. A contemporary of his in the Associates was the Burnley school teacher, Fred Marquis, who became Warden of the new Liverpool University Settlement in 1908. His political activities were to lead him to a peerage, as Lord Woolton, to the wartime Ministry of Food, and to the chairmanship of the Conservative Party. The departures of Mallon and Marquis to London and Liverpool respectively together with the resignations of Crompton and Marr from their Wardenships in 1909 brought some slackening in the Associates' activities. World War One took many of their young men, some of them permanently. By 1921, their numbers were down to 36, but five years later they reorganised, broadening their basis of membership and introducing a new body of Junior Associates.

World War II brought further decline then a revival

THE
TOYNBEE : DEBATING : SOCIETY.

Established March, 1896.

Officers of the Society.

President.
Prof. R. M. BURROWS, D.Litt.

Past Presidents.
E. T. CAMPAGNAC, M.A.
H. PILKINGTON TURNER, M.A., LL.B.
JAMES J. MALLON.
G. B. HERTZ, M.A., B.C.L.

Vice-Presidents.

W. BAILEY	C. PRIESTLEY
H. BURY	F. SCHOFIELD

Committee.

Miss S. ANDREWS	C. H. BRIERLEY
Mrs. C. H. BRIERLEY	W. MUTTER
Miss E. LEACH	R. H. RILEY

Hon. Sec. and Treas.
J. HARDMAN,
571, Gorton Road, Reddish, Stockport.

Toynbee Debating Society Programme - 1912/13

✏ Syllabus ✏

1912

Oct. 19. UNITED OPENING SOCIAL

Fawcett and Toynbee Debating Societies. Presidential Addresses by Miss L. M. KER and Professor R. M. BURROWS, D.Litt.

,, 26. **Home Rule**

Affirmative : F. SCHOFIELD
Negative : GERALD B. HERTZ, M.A., B.C.L.

Nov. 2. **The Labour Unrest**

E. J. HOOKWAY

,, 9. **Municipal Trading v. Private Enterprise**

Inter-Debate. Lancashire College Settlement.

,, 16. **The Rating of Land Values**

C. T. CAMPION

,, 23. **Would a General Industrial Strike against War be possible ?**

EDWARD E. DALE

,, 30. **Is Nature Cruel ? No !**

R. E. O'CALLAGHAN

Dec. 7. **That Unreal Democracy is the worst form of Tyranny**

Councillor MARGARET ASHTON

,, 14. **National Service**

Major STRACHAN

✏

VACATION

1913

Jan. 11. **The Ideal Commonwealth**

CHAS. PEACH

,, 18. **The Influence of the Press for good or evil**

J. CUMMING WALTERS

,, 25. **National Insurance and some of its effects**

WALTER DAVIES

Feb. 1. Prof. R. M. BURROWS, D.Litt.

,, 8. **The Relation of Political Economy to Morality and Practice**

R. B. FORRESTER, M.A.

,, 15. **Militarism**

A. F. JACK, M.A.

,, 22. **The reasonableness of Welsh Disestablishment**

ROBERT LEWIS

Mar. 1. Inter-Debate. Manchester University Sociological Society

,, 8. **Political Economy for Plain People**

C. H. PEARCE

,, 15. **Syndicalism**

A. A. PURCELL

,, 22. **Parliamentary Debate and Nomination of Officers**

,, 29. **Closing Social and Election of Officers**

in 1945 inspired by Richard Heath, the former leader of the Pilgrim Club. In the meantime, another group, the Mustard Club was introduced in 1937 for all resident and voluntary settlement workers.

Whether organised in groups of this sort, or coming as individuals, the Settlement has always relied heavily on, and gained greatly from, the involvement of voluntary workers, many of then students like those from Manchester University and Mather Training College whom Beatrice Rogers found so active in 1920 helping in play reading, French and handicraft classes, providing music for the At Homes, working at the Infant Welfare Centre and organising a scout troop. Fifty years later, Marie Williamson was also drawn into the whirlpool of this activity.

Fawcett Debating Society - social and political activities - 1908.

"I'd been to a meeting in the Roscoe Building at the University when I was back in Manchester, I'd seen an advert for doing children's holidays - it was when I was about 20 I did a training course together with a friend of mine and then other friends came along on other training courses and holidays. So I'd done a couple of holidays and the last one I did I couldn't face going back to the factory so I became a volunteer on the playscheme here in Beswick so that was it really. That would have been 1974. I worked as a full time volunteer for 10 months and more or less created my own job in that time and then I was employed when they managed to get funding." (Marie Williamson).

If social distinctions between volunteer and neighbour were noticed, they did not necessarily form a barrier to successful work.

"Rosemary (Verey) a helper, tried to have control of us. She was definitely different from us because she was educated and was going to help at the University (Settlement) not actually want of them. Ooh, she was dedicated. We got on well with her because she knew she was over us even though there was only a few years between us, we was 'Why can't we?' 'and all this, and ' 'Oh, let us'. She had to try and control us. We used to think that we'd shocked Mrs. Kidd with some of the things we'd come out with. She'd say to us 'You're villains. I don't know how I'm going to keep you on the straight and narrow.' I used to wonder why Mr. and Mrs. Kidd wanted to be there and I'd worry about how long they were going to stay. I do remember when there was talk about them going. I felt quite devastated and let down . I remember thinking could we really relate to them because they were a bit posher but you could, see? They were so kind, so gentle with us. If you'd had a bad day, you knew that if you went there, there was someone there who really cared." (Jacky Homer).

j. Academics

Professors and lecturers as well as students have always been closely associated with the Settlement, which was from the first a University Settlement. It was the meeting at Owens College in 1895 which launched the Settlement and the inspiration for it came from staff and students alike. The First Constitution laid down that the Principal of Owens College should be President of the Settlement "for the time being". A revised Constitution in 1901 relegated him to the post of Honorary Warden, but allowed for the election to the Settlement Council of three student members of Owens College Union and one from the Women's Union. It also allowed Owens Court of Governors to appoint one of the eight Settlement trustees when a successor was needed to the eminent history professor T. F. Tout. Tout had quickly succeeded T. C. Horsfall as chairman of the Settlement Council beginning a tradition maintained over the past century of senior academics playing a major role in the government of the Settlement. This was strengthened in 1919, when the Settlement and the Art Museum parted company and a new simplified constitution brought the Vice Chancellor, Sir Henry Miers, to the Presidency of the Settlement.

Such involvement has gone beyond the mere form of constitutional appointments. The early days of the Settlement witnessed a galaxy of academic talent giving lectures to the somewhat bemused Ancoats

Thomas Frederick Tout - Professor of history, Manchester University 1890 - 1925. Tout succeeded T.C.Horsfall as chairman of the Settlement Council, and played an active part in the early years in Ancoats.

neighbours. A series of Monday Popular Lectures in 1898 included the economists, Sydney Chapman and A. W. Flux on "England's Cotton Trade" and "The Burden of Taxation" respectively, P. J. Hartog on "The Chemistry of Common Things" and T. F. Tout on "Joan of Arc." Most popular of all, perhaps because of the accompanying lantern sides, was the zoologist S. J. Hickson relating his "Travels in the Malay

wonderful person. Her friendliness, modesty and I suppose humanity stood out like a beacon." (David Owen).

An annual fete was held at Ashburne Hall, the university's oldest women's hall of residence, in aid of Settlement Funds.

"Saturday's programme for the University Settlement

Archipelago." On a more practical level, professorial gardens in South Manchester were made available (not always, as has been, seen without incident) to visiting parties of Ancoats neighbours. Vice Chancellors and others dined at the Round House or at Ancoats Hall, and took part in the settlement's social activities.

"Mr. John Stopford, the then Vice Chancellor of the University, took a keen interest in the work of the Settlement and would visit on occasions during the year, as well as attend quite a number of special activities. Many other quite well known people also visited and were entertained at Ancoats Hall. I still remember vividly the visit of Dame Sybil Thorndyke, the actress, to Ancoats Hall. I have never, before or since, met such a

---

MANCHESTER UNIVERSITY SETTLEMENT
AND ART MUSEUM
IN CONJUNCTION WITH THE
WORKERS' EDUCATIONAL ASSOCIATION
MANCHESTER BRANCH

History and the War

A COURSE OF LECTURES

WILL BE GIVEN IN THE

ANCOATS HALL, ANCOATS

(EVERY STREET), ON

Friday Evenings, *Nov.* 6, 13, 20, 27

BY

G. S. VEITCH, M.A., LITT.D.

(Lecturer in Modern History, University of Liverpool).

Subjects

I.	November 6	- -	THE TRIPLE ALLIANCE
II.	November 13	- -	THE TRIPLE ENTENTE
III.	November 20	- -	THE EASTERN QUESTION
IV.	November 27	- -	THE PRESENT CRISIS

LECTURES TO COMMENCE AT 8-0 P.M. PROMPT
DISCUSSION AND QUESTIONS INVITED

PRICES OF TICKETS - - COURSE, 6d.; SINGLE LECTURE, 2d.

is a blend of well tried traditions and creative intelligence. On the conservative side one feels safe in placing the stalls and the 'white elephant' stall in particular. Refreshments by the University refectory make the best of both worlds. There are strawberries and a milk-bar. Gymnastic, acrobatic and morris dancing

All in a good cause! Students collecting money for the Settlement (and other charities) in Market Street Manchester.
- Rag Day, 1948.

displays, conjuring and the open air carnival dance are restful for the spectator. A spelling bee, though the craze is a revival, must be reckoned among the new, especially as the competitive sides are the University staff and students. The Hazel Grove twins who promise a pound note to anyone who can make them laugh or speak are undeniably original though one is prepared to learn that the idea comes from the Old Testament, Boccaccio or one of the Greeks. All this in the restful modern stateliness of Ashburne Hall grounds needs only a fine afternoon to make a happy time and - what is equally important - a financially successful one." (Manchester Guardian June 17th 1938).

Such events, organised by the University Women's Club continued until recent times. By the mid 1980's however, Women's Club membership had declined and it was decided in 1986 no longer to hold the

Sir John Stopford, Vice Chancellor, Manchester University - 1934.

annual Spring Fair, but to ask individual members too make donations to the Settlement instead. The Students' Union were even more active in the area of fund raising, giving part of the proceeds of their annual Rag Day to the Settlement as well as providing a good deal of practical help and involvement.

"The Playcentre we used to go to was always run by students. The students used to come from the University and organise games and all this and take us out on these walks and train rides say from London Road to Gorton. When we were on school holidays we were never on the streets, we always had something to do and it was mainly at the Settlement." (Joan Seaton).

As the University grew, however, there were many of its members, staff and student, who had no knowledge of its Settlement, nor of Ancoats, Beswick or Gorton. "What will you do?" enquired the Manchester University Union News Bulletin of its readers in 1934.

"Help in any way you can, and remember the Wardens ask you to come down and see them some time. M.C.T.D. run 51 trams primarily for this purpose." (M.U.U. News Bulletin 7 Dec 4th 1934).

Academics too needed constant reminders. In 1956, the chairman of the Settlement's Executive Committee sent a letter to all University staff not contributing to the "University's own charity" and proposing that each lecturer subscribe £2 : 2s and each professor £3 : 3s annually. In March , 1993, a similar "begging letter" from the chairman arrived in staff mail boxes, pointing out that "the Settlement's

THE MANCHESTER

UNIVERSITY SETTLEMENT

ANNUAL REPORT

1919-1920

The Settlement Office is in the Art Museum at the junction of Every St. and Great Ancoats St. Cars between the University and Miller St. (Route 51) pass the door. From Piccadilly the Clayton and Edge Lane cars (Route 27) come to within three minutes' walk (alight at the Ancoats Lane corner of Pollard Street)

OFFICE AT
ANCOATS HALL
MANCHESTER
TEL.: CENT. 6915

RESIDENCE:
20 EVERY STREET
ANCOATS

work is less widely known in the University than it deserves to be," and suggesting that "an annual sum of £100 and upwards might be appropriate." Meanwhile student activity is making a welcome return to its tradition of funding and helping.

"There is no holiday this year but what may possibly happen, students from the University have volunteered to do a camp in October with children from this area. In a sense it's a bit like reverting back, using students again. There are students on the Management Committee now." (Marie Williamson).

Academics from all disciplines have been actively involved in Settlement business over the past hundred years, and the chairs of Settlement Council have ranged all the way from a professor of history (T. F. Tout) to a professor of geography (B. T. Robson). Nevertheless, the professionalisation of social work in this period and the growing interest in social investigation has led to a particularly close link between the Settlement and the applied social sciences. G. K. Grierson, appointed Warden in 1913, was a university lecturer in social science, teaching courses which "include lectures on and the acquirement of, practical acquaintance with social problems and conditions." He was, the annual report informed its readers, gradually forming a library relating to the subject at the Settlement. In 1926, when the University created a new Department of Social Study, it appointed the new Warden, Hilda Cashmore, to the post of Supervisor of Practical Work within it. The Settlement took its students, as well as those from other universities, into residence to undertake their practical social work training. In the 1950's and 1960's, the presence of Brian and Barbara Rodgers in the University's Department of Social Administration greatly strengthened the links between the Settlement

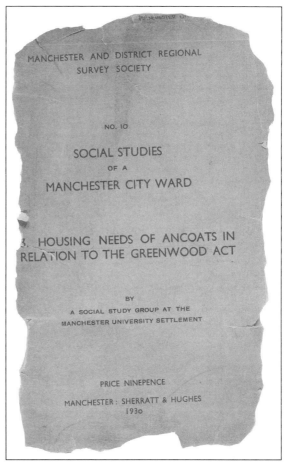

Social Research at the Settlement - cover of report by Social Study Group.

and this area of the University's work. Brian Rodgers played an active role in settlement work, joining the Manchester University Settlement Council in 1947, and becoming acting chair, and later vice-chair of the Executive Committee in 1952. In 1956, he was elected chair of the British Association of Residential

Diagrams showing sources of income of poor families in Ancoats - from the Settlement Survey of 1937/8.

Settlements, the central organisation of the British settlement house movement, and represented it at the International Conference of Settlements in Berlin in the same year.

Social studies in the academic context involved research as well as teaching and training. Settlement houses not only provided institutional bases for the training of social workers, but also laboratories or observation platforms from which investigation of the social problems affecting the inner city could be carried out. In 1899, the Settlement's annual report expressed its regret that little work of this sort was being done since "residents at the Settlement have peculiar facilities for being acquainted with the actual conditions of life around them." Two years later it

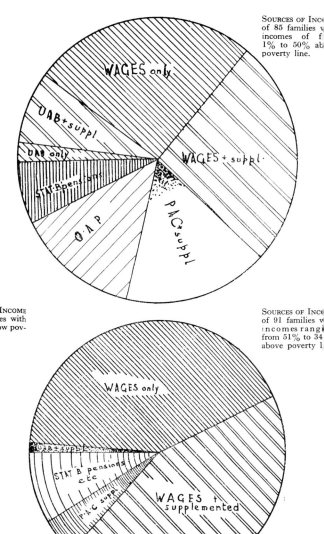

SOURCES OF INCO
of 85 families v
incomes of f
1% to 50% ab
poverty line.

Abbreviations.—
UAB—Allowance from Unemployment Assistance Board : PAC—Allowance from Public Assistance Committee: STAT. B.—Statutory Benefit under Unemployment Acts : OAP—Old Age Pensions :

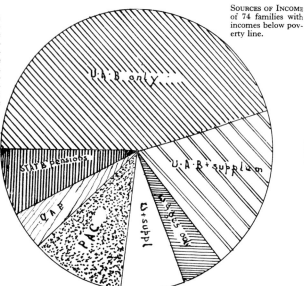

SOURCES OF INCOME
of 74 families with incomes below poverty line.

SOURCES OF INC
of 91 families v
incomes rangi
from 51% to 34
above poverty l

chester City Council

)CIAL SERVICE IN MUNICIPAL HOUSING AREAS

Help of the University Settlement

BOUR ALDERMAN'S BITTER ATTACK ON "INVESTIGATORS"

eral topics of public interest debated at the meeting of ester City Council yesterday, gh there was, as some members sted, an electioneering note in a of the speeches, and the sitting rolonged into the late afternoon sequence.

n and 'bus fares, the powers of nance Committee, and the ques- f encouraging the community- ng work of the University Settle- on municipal housing estates in w flats were among the subjects d.

Housing Committee reported that acceded to the application of the ester University Settlement that a nominated by the settlement be granted the tenancy of a three- flat at Kennet House in which to h a community centre under the ent. Kennet House is the new f the group of 180 flats at Smedley o which families from houses in t slum-clearance areas have been red.

Alderman Titt's Attack

man Titt moved that the decision be sent back for reconsideration pressed the hope that at the next meeting they would hear that irregularity" had not been pro- with. He claimed that the flats n built exclusively for the accom- on of people dispossessed by slum es and that it was wrong, while Is of families still needed houses, ne flat to someone nominated by versity Settlement who was not in a house.

this point the Alderman pro- to speak slightingly of the social fare work of the settlement, and he pleaded with the council "for ake" not to give room to these ointed social investigators who

went about dissecting and vivisecting the life of the working classes.

Councillor William Collingson formally seconded and then Alderman Joseph Binns, speaking with considerable feeling and as one having experience of what Settlement workers had done on the Newton Heath Estate to establish a community life and spirit, repudiated the suggestion that the lives of the tenants would be spied upon and declared that the whole object of the Settlement workers would be to start movements that would bring pleasure, learning, and companionship and to leave those move- ments entirely at the disposal and under the control of the tenants. Such inspira- tion and assistance as the Settlement would give would be found—as had been the case elsewhere—invaluable in bring- ing together tenants who had been collected from the four quarters of the city.

"Uplift Not Wanted"

Councillors Larrad, Regan, and Gorman, speaking from the Labour benches, also opposed the Housing Com- mittee's recommendation. Councillor Larrad said that their poverty was the real crime of these dispossessed slum- dwellers and they did not need uplifting. Alternatively, if they did need it they would not have it. Councillor Gorman objected that no outside body should be given the right to "nominate" a tenant or tenants for a municipal house, and that if the University Settlement were given the right then it could not be denied to the Salvation Army or some other religious or political body which considered it was doing good. Councillor Regan talked about the other tenants being "insulted" by having Settlement workers quartered among them.

"Every possible prejudice," said Councillor Wright Robinson, speak- ing from the Labour benches, "has been introduced into this debate by Alderman Titt and Councillor Larrad. It must be common knowledge that on every one of these large housing estates thousands of families, uprooted from their own sur- roundings, have been thrown together in an entirely new environment, and in

Burnage, Wythenshawe, and elsewhere it has been absolutely essential to form some kind of community organisation so that the people may get to know each other and may cater for their own social needs and amenities." That was what was intended for Kennet House, and he resented the suggestion that there would be any "nosing into people's private affairs."

Councillor A. P. Simon, a member of the executive and also of the Council of the University Settlement, expressed profound distress that opposition in such terms should have come from Labour members, who were making a task that was already a very real task into one increasingly difficult by introducing considerations of class which did not and should not exist. He believed that the Act under which the slum-dwellers were being rehoused did, in fact, con- template some such provision as a com- munity centre for them. If it had been difficult for people on the new housing estates to coalesce and build up a happy communal life without assistance, then it would be still more difficult in the case of those brought together in one great building divided into flats.

Tribute to Settlement

Alderman Walker asked the opponents of the recommendation whether they sincerely believed that in one instance where the University Settlement had been at work on a municipal estate a vote could be obtained in favour of its exclusion. Give it one year in Kennet House and the same result would follow.

Alderman Sir Miles Mitchell, making the formal reply on the debate as chair- man of the Housing Committee, objected to the misrepresentations, prejudice, and exaggerations which had been freely introduced. He claimed that the com- mittee had discharged to the satisfaction of the council the duty it had had for fifteen or sixteen years of managing the municipal housing estates, and he paid high tribute to the assistance which the committee had had in this task from the University Settlement and its voluntary workers. It was work that had been of immeasurable benefit to the people living on the estates, and he believed that its extension in rehousing was essential to the complete success of that great experiment. No tenant of a slum-clearance house would be kept out of a house in consequence, and no remission from the usual rent would be made to the Settlement.

When Alderman Titt's amendment was put to the vote the Lord Mayor, upon a show of hands, said that it was so plainly defeated that there was no necessity to take a count.

338

reported with some satisfaction that "the Settlement is slowly if surely acquiring the character of a bureau of social information." This probably reflects the influence of T. R. Marr whose study of housing conditions in Manchester and Salford with its radical schemes for developing municipal housing appeared in 1904. As an associate, resident and men's Warden after 1901, Marr encouraged residents and associates to bring together for analysis the information they obtained from neighbours and their children in clubs and classes, and on visits to homes in Ancoats. R. C. K. Ensor, in 1903, used his experience in working for Santa Fina to collate and analyse the ages, geographical distribution and nature of the disablement of its members in the neighbourhood. In January and February, 1904, the Settlement Associates made a house to house survey to discover the extent of unemployment in Ancoats. They found that 5.4% of the

"Nosing into peoples' affairs." Another view of social investigation -October 1935.

MANCHESTER   UNIVERSITY   SETTLEMENT

ANCOATS: A STUDY OF A CLEARANCE AREA

Report of a Survey made in 1937-1938

Foreword by the
Right Honourable LORD WOOLTON, P.C.

From a woodcut by **THE ROUND HOUSE.** *Margaret Pilkington.*

PRICE 1/6

encouraged by its Warden, T. R. Marr, led to the Settlement's being regarded as a centre of expertise on which social investigators, local and national, could call. In 1913, the London based Ratan Tata Foundation which was carrying out a study of the effect of the Trades Boards Act of 1909 in regulating wages and working conditions in the sweated trades, turned to the Settlement to gather and analyse the evidence on this subject in the Manchester area. Four years earlier, the Settlement's Poor Man's Lawyer Department had submitted evidence to the Royal Commission on Marriage and Divorce with regard to the nature of the marriage problems which neighbours had brought to it, and in 1914 the Settlement monitored and reported upon rising food and other prices in Manchester for a Government concerned that inflation might undermine morale at the time of national emergency.

In the 1930's, a Social Survey Group, organised by Edward Allen, was based at Every Street to take advantage of the detailed but disinterested view which Settlement residents and workers had of the social problems of Ancoats. Sub-groups were formed to investigate particular problems of health, housing, the siting of industry and the movement of boys from school to work. Many of these investigations were published in a series entitled <u>Social Studies of a Manchester City Ward</u>.

A Settlement resident, J. D. Inman, carried out a survey of poverty in Miles Platting and published its results in a book, <u>Poverty and Housing Conditions in</u>

population, many of them young people, were unemployed, and , perhaps more importantly, that many others were working short time or were in casual employment. Such research activity, strongly

Typical Ancoats backs. - Houses scheduled for demolition.

a Manchester Ward, which added a Manchester dimension to a number of regional studies charting the poverty of Britain between the wars.

With the beginning of slum clearance, the experience of Settlement workers and neighbours both in Ancoats and on new estates like Wilbraham Road or Gorton, provided excellent material for a study of the social problems which large movements of people from inner city to council estate would create. In 1936, the Carnegie Trust helped to finance such a study directed by one of the Settlement's Wardens, Jean Wyatt. Its first stage, published in 1938, showed

City of Manchester. New Cross clearance orders Nos. 1 to 5, 1957. New Cross Housing compulsory purchase order, 1937.

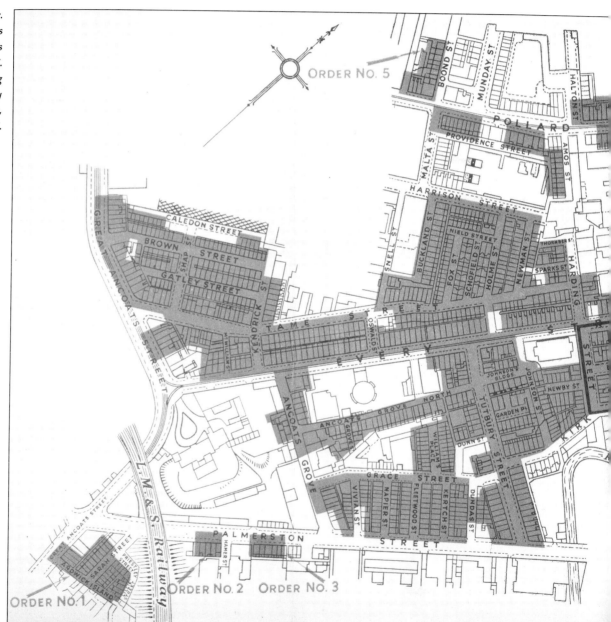

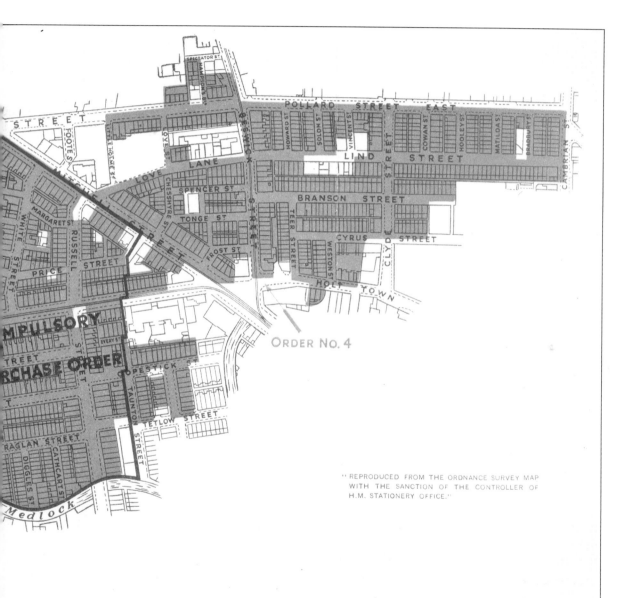

ORDER No. 4

" REPRODUCED FROM THE ORDNANCE SURVEY MAP
WITH THE SANCTION OF THE CONTROLLER OF
H.M. STATIONERY OFFICE."

Scale: 208·33 feet to an inch

Children's Literacy Scheme - the project, with a staff of four, involved working with small groups of children with difficulties, both in local schools and at Aidan's.

clearly the deep rooted family and neighbourly connections of Ancoats people and their concern at being split up and moved to new homes. This concern was increased by the long time periods which elapsed between scheduling areas for demolition and the work of clearance being carried out.

The second world War disrupted the second part of the survey, but in 1942 a Survey Committee was set up at Gorton to investigate the Belle Vue estate and to try to find out something about the neighbours' views of their new surroundings. This survey was published in 1943.

After 1945, the research activities of the Settlement seem to have diminished, and, in a report on the Settlement's activities in 1964, Isobel Griffiths from the London School of Economics reminded members that a university settlement should conduct continuous research into social needs and that a definite programme of research should be drawn up and finance allocated for that purpose.

Despite this belief that the Settlement, like a University department, should make social research a prominent and separate aspect of its mission, the idea was by no means uncontroversial. It could interfere with the central settlement ideal of working together with the neighbours resident in the area on a mutual and equal basis of co-operation to improve the quality of life. Social surveys might lead to working class neighbours feeling like microbes placed beneath the microscopes of clever, middle class academics.

During a debate on housing in Manchester City

M. U. S.

CHILDREN'S LITERACY SCHEME

Council in 1935, Alderman Titt criticised the decision to grant a tenancy in a new flat to a worker seconded by the Settlement. He pleaded with council, not "for God's sake to give room to these self appointed social investigators who went about dissecting and vivisecting the lives of the working class." Although

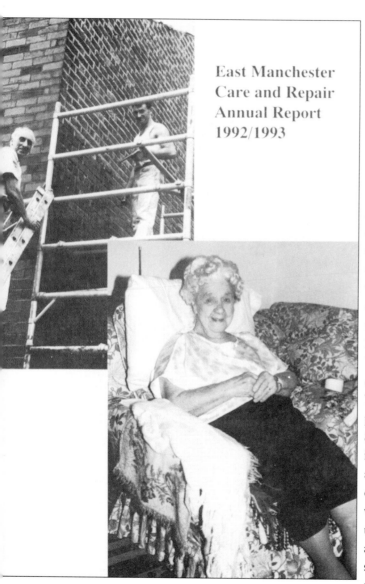

East Manchester
Care and Repair
Annual Report
1992/1993

he was quickly silenced by other Labour councillors, and the amendment he proposed defeated, the alderman had a point. Could you live on close terms with your neighbour and at the same time analyse the contents of her dustbin?

This narrow line between neighbourliness and academic research proved from the first to be a difficult one for university settlements like Manchester's to tread. Perhaps this has been solved in more recent times by following the settlement tradition of pioneering new schemes of work within and with the community. The Children's Literacy Scheme of the later 1970's which led to the Settlement's being by 1980 one of the leading units in the country for tackling the problems of teenage literacy: the Beswick Women's Health project; the Credit Union; the Care and Repair Scheme for the elderly, and, most recently, the East Manchester Young People's Housing Project, have been practical initiatives launched from the Settlement but with a view to not merely involving local people, but giving them control and empowering them to regenerate a depressed community. Such schemes generate information which can be run through the computers of university social science departments, but they are concerned with activity not with passive social research. They are following the best practice of the settlement ideal.

Care & Repair Scheme at work (above) with a satisfied client (below). The scheme aims to provide the elderly with technical and financial advice on improvements or repairs to their homes and co-operates with local authority, local builders and community welfare organisations to achieve this.

A major problem throughout the Settlement's hundred year history has been that of raising the finance to fund its multiple activities. Maintenance of buildings and their furnishings, and the payment of salaries, however modest, always constituted a major call on the Settlement's shallow coffers. Its wide range of work with neighbours of all ages and conditions has been a great strength, but in narrow financial terms it has often proved a weakness. Unlike more specialist charities, the Settlement has difficulty in targeting its appeals. Though an emergency appeal in 1978 succeeded in overcoming a financial crisis, an appeal to industry in the following year brought a poor response, netting only £500 and 30 footballs!

At first, like other charities in nineteenth century Manchester, the Settlement depended heavily upon the annual subscriptions, most of them ranging between 10/- and £5, of its supporters. Fund raising events such as the Students' Union's annual Rag Day or the Ashburne Hall bazaar provided welcome lumps of annual income, but their amounts could not be forecast in advance with any confidence. Special events like the Manchester premiere of the film, <u>A Taste of Honey</u>, in 1962 which raised £500 for Settlement funds were also welcome but rare occasions.

Fees from residents and lodgers for board at Ancoats Hall were an important source of income in the first fifty years of the Settlement's existence, although in some years expenditure exceeded income. In recent years, the University has helped its Settlement with an annual grant of £4,000.

Chapter Four

FINANCE

Fund Raising Event - 1961. Unfortunately such star studded events have not been very frequent.

The Ancoats neighbours also supported the Settlement financially. It was not a relief giving institution. Those attending clubs and classes paid a subscription of a few pence a week. Admission fees were charged for dances, plays and concerts, and small sums were collected weekly to help with the cost of Settlement holidays and outings. The Recreation Room and later the refurbished Round House were hired out for local events, and other organisations hired rooms there in which to carry out their work.

With the increasing role of government, national and local, in social work in the twentieth century, the Settlement was able to obtain grants for carrying out work for which the state had become responsible.

Growing concern for the aged brought the Settlement a grant of £500 from the city's welfare services committee in 1962 to provide a basement kitchen and service lift at the Round House. This meant that a restaurant for elderly neighbours could be opened serving hot lunches at 1/- on 5 days in a week. Note could be kept of those who attended regularly so that unexplained absentees could

A CHARITY PREMIÈRE

IN AID OF

The Manchester University Settlement

IN THE PRESENCE OF THE STARS

AT

The New Oxford Theatre, Oxford Street, Manchester

3 p.m. Sunday, 22nd October, 1961

Programme **2/6**

be visited to ensure that they were not ill or housebound for some other reason.

Such finance however often came in the shape of grants over a fixed period of time for projects such as the pioneering and highly successful Children's Literacy Scheme. This has meant not only a constant need to review programmes with a view to applications for funding renewal, but also dependence upon the ever changing policies of government as far as social funding is concerned. In the financial crisis of the late 1970's, the City Council's policy committee deferred payment of grants to the Settlement until a working party had investigated the state of its finances. Fortunately its review proved satisfactory, and the Settlement's grant was increased to take account of inflation. Nevertheless, like many late 20th century voluntary institutions, the Settlement had become dependent upon the goodwill of the state to an extent which its founders never envisaged.

"The children's literacy scheme started up in the late '70's and it managed to get funding from Manpower Services initially and then from Inner Cities Funding and it continued until two or three years ago until funding cuts. Pat's funding was due to go last year as it was a joint funding between Health Authority and Social Services and it was time expired so it was due to go in any case, so all that's gone." (Marie Williamson).

For larger items of capital expenditure, the Settlement has often benefited from the generosity of individuals. The Alice Bickham bequest refurbished the Round House in the 1920's, and John Zochonis provided substantial aid for the building of the new Aidans in the early 1980's. Nor did all such funding come from outside the community.

"Dad had to go round all the Boys' clubs to try and get money for the scheme. (Pilgrim Club). He went to one ice cream man in Ancoats. He noticed the lad was bringing a pound note with him every time (he came to a Settlement boys' club). Well a pound note was a lot of money. So dad thought he would visit this chap. He told him where he had come from and what his name was and the chap said 'Open that cupboard and take a handful.' Dad said 'Don't you mind how much I take?'

He said 'No, no I don't believe in banks.' He was Italian you see. The boy was going to the Settlement because, of course, they had the activities that kiddies want." (Stanley Heath).

Unfortunately such welcome generosity whether from Altrincham or Ancoats were isolated occurrences which could not be planned for. From its beginnings the Settlement's annual reports give a picture of a hard pressed treasurer ever struggling to make ends meet. Most serious have been the years when hand to mouth management and cheese paring was not enough, and the Settlement faced the very real prospect of bankruptcy and failure. In 1925, Every Street and the Round House were on the point of being handed over to the city when an energetic public appeal and the windfall of the Bickham bequest saved the Settlement and restored the Round House. In 1939, some members of the executive committee were "inclined to go ahead in faith" whilst others thought that "to go bankrupt in a few months would be worse than to close down in good order." Fortunately the faithful were in the majority. In 1977, the bank foreclosed on the Settlement's overdraft, and there was again a very real possibility of closure. Sale of the Moss Side properties and an emergency appeal rescued it once again, although only after careful scrutiny of its finances by the city.

After one hundred years, the problem is unresolved. The assumption that "someone" - city, government, or university - must fund the Settlement is a comfortable illusion.

Manchester Art Museum & University Settlement.

———••———

ANCOATS HALL,
EVERY STREET,
MANCHESTER,
January, 1909.

DEAR SIR, or MADAM,

I beg to remind you that your subscription to the above is now due. At foot you will find stated the amount you contributed last year, and I shall be glad if you will send your subscription as early as possible to THE WARDEN at the above address.

A copy of the last Annual Report is enclosed, from which you will see that the many activities associated with Ancoats Hall are still being carried on, and that there is, in consequence, still the same need for financial assistance.

Yours truly,

JOHN W. GRAHAM,
Hon. Treasurer.

George Unwin, Manchester University's first professor of economic history, did not share the enthusiasm of his fellow historian, T. F. Tout, for university settlements. They were, in his view, "an easy way to heaven" for the wealthy middle classes who came from comfortable homes in Bowdon or Alderley Edge to do penance in Ancoats for the alleged sins of capitalism. The Labour leader, George Lansbury, held similar views. Work at a settlement house, he pointed out, was often a preliminary to high political or professional office in later life. The middle class settler gained much more than did the working class settled. Settlements have been seen as the fag end of Victorian charity and religious idealism, faintly ridiculous institutions for "do gooders" trying to bring cultural uplift to a largely indifferent working class. Historians have largely ignored settlements, with the exception of some of the high profile London ones, notably Toynbee Hall.

Subscription reminder - 1909.

General practitioners in the field of social work, settlements spearheaded no single minded, highly publicised campaign for social reform. They preferred to experiment, initiate and then pass on the initiative to other organisations, public or private. After World War Two, affluence and the growth of state welfare led many to assume that their role was over. Post war planning destroyed the communities in which they had worked. The idea of residence all but disappeared by the 1970s. Many settlements closed or were transformed into other types of community institution.

Manchester University Settlement has survived. Its location was transferred, the Round House and Ancoats Hall are gone, but, as these pages and pictures show, it has kept its faith that by investing in people, it can bring hope and renewal to a still deprived area of a great city.

Reading through the archives and old minute books of the Settlement, thoughts of "then as now" came into my head. The shortage of funding, the plea for access to facilities from a mix of groups (the artists seeking quiet contemplation and the children seeking a noisy activity), a committed, enthusiastic yet exhausted staff, a willing bunch of volunteers, a skilled and supportive management committee and a building that endlessly leaks, cracks and demands expensive heating.

After a boom time of funding in the 70's and 80's, the voluntary sector has faced dramatic cuts to its budget in the 90's. Funders now want to see their name displayed on exciting and innovative projects - yet they are unwilling to fund the very organisations that develop the projects that offer them accommodation, feasibility studies and management and support for the staff. The Settlement works on the concept that the "apple needs its core" and this has recently been verified by a study carried out at the London School of Economics.

Staff help has become part of the jargon. Yet again, without the resources of the Settlement to provide a meeting space, telephones, stationery, advice and above all professional staff then staff help groups cannot flourish.

Despite these financial constraints the Settlement is thriving and providing a number of projects which ensures that local people are able to improve the quality of their lives and to reduce the effects of poverty. In the early 1990's Manchester expected to

Chapter Five

win the bid for the 2000 Olympic Games, on a site just half a mile from our current site. The bid failed and the infrastructural changes, new roads, sports facilities, office complex and helicopter pad have provided none of the social support so much needed by the people of the area. Indeed they feel cheated at having had their hopes of employment, recreational facilities, better shopping and school facilities raised - only to see the land and road developers and large wealthy companies beat a hasty retreat from East Manchester when the profit motive was removed.

We seek to regenerate people. The majority of investment in the inner cities is around improvements to infrastructure and to attracting large business investment. We want the local communities to benefit from this investment, to gain the jobs, the improved environment, the leisure facilities. It is pointless to provide roads, hypermarkets, office blocks and sports stadiums if the local population cannot afford to enjoy the facilities, or cannot gain employment within them.

The Settlement is a genuine partnership between the University and the local people. The university is able to assist in the development of projects, advise on issues such as planning and law, provide students and staff to work alongside projects and to carry out research. In return the grass roots knowledge and experience complements academic achievement and can influence policy makers.

The Content of our Work

The communities have been decimated by unemployment for the past 30 years. Currently 34% of the adult population available for work are unemployed, 80% of young men between the ages of 16 - 19 are unemployed. We are now looking at the second and third generations of families who are unfamiliar with the concept of work. Apathy is rife and many lack motivation towards initiatives which can improve (although never solve) on issues of unemployment.

An underclass is developing

People who live in local authority housing which is cold, damp and unsafe as a result of the government's restriction on local government spending.

People who suffer from poor health at a time when the National Health Service is being starved of cash and expected to work in a free market economy.

People who suffer from stress and mental health problems (25% of the community is currently receiving drugs or treatment related to mental health).

People living under fear of crime, particularly burglary to satisfy the growing drug dependency culture - insurance companies will either charge exorbitant rates to insure, or will not insure at all in certain areas.

People struggling on low incomes where shopping facilities are scarce, where there is no choice between stores or their products. Shops selling basic children's clothing, shoes and affordable foods have closed down. The market (a shopping and social place) has been closed for the development of a new ring road.

People trying to balance low budgets. For those aged between 16 and 19 there are no benefits payable and families are forced to exclude their own children. A single person receives £42.00 per week on which to live (at time of writing a loaf of bread costs 84 pence, a pint of milk 50 pence, a bag of sugar 48 pence, a tin of baked beans 32 pence, six eggs 59 pence and jar of coffee £2.10 pence and a pack of butter 74 pence).

There are areas in East Manchester with no banking facilities, and the electricity and gas services will not provide outlets for their pre payment cards as they feel they will be robbed. People travel into the city centre for these cards at a cost of £1.60 on the bus.

People cannot afford to run their own cars, yet the public transport system has been destroyed by privatisation. Travel to work is difficult by public transport, it is unsafe at night and unclean.

And What of the Future??

Funding as ever is a prime concern. In order to support our projects and the wider community we have put together a strategy for growth and development, which includes a community outreach worker; a fundraising boost via the appointment of a professional fundraiser; enhancement and development of the projects which currently operate; additional trust funding to be supported by the student union; a give as you live scheme for students and a give as you earn scheme for academics and other staff at the university.

The business plan shows viable organisation which can grow into its second century of community and anti poverty work; we are now reliant on additional support from the University in order to unlock promised matching funds from a number of trusts and private individuals. None the less, we are a charity and the work we provide, although vital to local people, cannot be measured in the present market economy. Compulsive competitive tendering could mean the end of our ability to respond to the needs of the local community, if local government do not see that work as a part of their agenda. It is vital, therefore, that we remain truly a part of an independent sector.

Government is keen on the term "partnership"– aimed at releasing private sector funding into what was once seen as public sector responsibility - capital investment in education, local regeneration initiatives, transport and preservation of the urban environment. Clearly, working in partnership may achieve more than isolation, but the voluntary sector can never match either private companies or local authorities in their wealth or resources, staff and expertise, or even status for many of our leaders. Thus we have to beg to join in any discussions, planning or issues which may ultimately affect our own organisation or our constituents. Equality is not really on the table!

The plans for the coming three years include provision of a local multi disciplinary sports and community facilities in partnership with the private sector, banks and the local authority.

Development of a foyer housing project which will provide temporary accommodation for young homeless people; offer them construction training skills; and move on to actual employment renovating or building their own homes. Thus we would expect to house, train, employ and provide permanent homes for 50 people per year.

Care and repair has been supported by the Department of Environment to develop into new geographical areas and is increasing its staff to improve more homes and lives for older people. We now work in Beswick, Bradford, Clayton, Lightbown and Monsall. Technical and casework skills are to be enhanced by the employment of a handy person team, who will carry out the small but essential additional tasks needed, from painting and decorating to fitting new gas appliances, fixing the garden gate and putting up shelving.

The community project is applying for funding to establish a local community chest - which will fund self help projects and get new initiatives off the ground. This may include use of premises, trainers or creche support. The work will be overseen by the Settlement as a registered charity and we will involve the local community in making decisions on policy and actual grant giving.

Effort is being put into the development of outward bound courses for young people in an attempt to equip them for training and the possibilities of the world of work; crime is a direct result of unemployment and the obvious wealth of some individuals and the widening gap between the haves and have nots is contributing to the break down in society.

So What Are We Doing Now??

Care and repair provides an effective and caring service for older people who wish to improve their houses. Grants for the building improvements are obtained, builders selected, plans drawn up in consultation with the client and we will even arrange temporary accommodation for both the clients and their pets.

The young people's housing project has given a group of young people training and qualifications in construction at a local college and the ability to work with architects and a housing association to convert redundant terraced properties into flats in which they themselves now live. The group have been supported in their personal development and gained skills in budgeting, decision making, food preparation, job search.

The Beswick and Bradford community project works with the community to provide a meeting place and network for local self help groups. These include parent and toddler, keep fit, healthy eating, teaching those recently out of care to cook for themselves, a youth project, Duke of Edinburgh's scheme, Somali group, dance and excerise and is working towards development of a community forum.

The credit union is defeating the loan sharks (people who offer loans at high rates of interest to those who could not raise money on the usual commercial market) by providing a savings and loan facility run by the local community for the local community.

The tenants' and residents' association is a forum for the discussion of local issues and works alongside the local authority to improve the built environment.

Local pensioners meet for both social activity and to campaign of behalf of our older population.

Young people and children are catered for with playschemes, an after school club, holidays and outward bound activities.

A recycling project is improving the environment, training volunteers and raising funds to expand its area of work.

The womens' health programme run classes on physical well being, stress and preventative health care.

In 1995, the Settlement faces the challenge of survival in a cold climate of change which has reproduced many of the appalling circumstances of one hundred years ago, has added new and often more unpleasant situations, and has miserably failed to offer coherent solutions.

Social and economic needs in an area like East Manchester are as acute now as at any stage since the foundation of the Settlement. Indeed, if anything, they are worse now than in the past. It is true that, during the hey-day of Britain's industrial power, workers faced the uncertainty of economic fluctuation, but now the loss of a manufacturing base has left large parts of our big cities facing grim and apparently long-term prospects of joblessness, of poverty, of poor housing and of creaking social service provision. East Manchester once provided the backbone of much of the city's manufacturing activity - textiles, iron and steel, chemicals - its market has now been decimated. The results are only too apparent: acres of derelict and abandoned land; empty and forlorn buildings; a public housing programme that appears to have stopped in its tracks; the closure of activities, like shops, which depend on local trade. And the social immiseration is equally evident from the statistics of the 1991 census which show the extent of joblessness, of inadequate housing, of ill-health, of poor education. Rising standards of living for the majority have been bought at the expense of too large a minority of the population both within and without urban conglomerations. The problem of the

PROFESSOR
BRIAN ROBSON

CHAIR OF SETTLEMENT COUNCIL

A CHALLENGE TOO FAR?

next century is how to heal the gaping wounds being caused by this social polarisation and how to prevent their re-occurrence.

Fifty years ago there was probably an increasing consensus that the state should have increasing, and eventual total, responsibility for such ameliorative action. Voluntary agencies like the Settlement were expected to fade with time and government action. They are indeed struggling, but the need for them continues to grow.

However, the successes and failures of the Welfare State followed by the revival of rugged individualism since 1979, have meant a great change in the context in which voluntary agencies like the Settlement now operate. In the 1960s and '70s, the voluntary sector went through a process of professionalising itself, employing paid professional workers whose jobs and projects were funded by a range of programmes supported both by central and local government: not least through the Urban Programme and through the various training programmes which introduced new initials like CP, ET, YTS. The corollary of financial support was, of course, that agencies increasingly responded to the funding opportunities set by outside funders and thereby ran the risk of losing the independence and innovativeness that has long been a strength of voluntary agencies. Now, the relationship between the funders and agencies has been formalised through service-level contracts which spell out the nature of the service to be provided and there is increasing difficulty in finding support for the general

'core' functions which hold the agencies together. This difficulty has been compounded by the ending of the government's Urban Programme and the increasing financial squeeze on the finances of the local authority.

The Settlement has suffered particularly in losing local authority support for its 'core' fund. The £4000 provided annually by the University is no substitute for the £60,000 formerly provided by the City Council! The Settlement has been dynamic in attracting funds from trusts, foundations and from the City Council for range of diverse projects. For example it provides support to a number of grass-roots self-help groups - pensioner clubs, recycling, holiday play, a credit union, a community co-operative and the like - using its premises as an important local facility. It has also developed specific new projects largely focused on housing - like a care and repair scheme, a young people's housing project and a foyer system - and partly on stated local needs - such as an after-school play group, an outward-bound programme, literacy and numeracy projects and women's health issues. In the setting up and the running of all such projects, the core of the Settlement offers advice, management expertise, training support and general administration.

New innovative projects can usually attract support; the core service are always more difficult to fund. Since it is harder to obtain and retain 'core' funding there is a grave danger that the Settlement will become like the old trees which line that street of suburban Manchester and about which there is so much agonising by comfortable citizens. They may appear flourishing and healthy, but the decay at their roots and their general neglect is only revealed when one falls on some unfortunate's roof. The Settlement provides the roots for the sturdy trunk from which the projects branch out: without funding for its core it will be unable to survive. Currently the generosity of a former Chairman of the University Council, John Zochonis, and a one-off sum from the University has rescued the Settlement from oblivion in its centennial year, but the need for secure long-term funding is omni-present and acute.

Individual donations are an important plank to sustain this work. We hope that staff and students in the University will offer regular financial support as well as offering their services in support of the Settlement's work. It may well be that the organisation needs renaming. 'University Settlement' is not perhaps a satisfactory phrase for the Millennium, but at least let us show that the members of the University of Manchester are no less a caring and active part of our parent city in 1995 than in 1895.